10 STEPS ON THE STAIRWAY TO HEAVEN ON EARTH

#LearnFromMyMistakes

CALEB BERNSTEIN

ISBN: 148201565X
ISBN-13: 9781482015652

TO ALL THOSE WHO INSPIRED AND SUPPORTED
ME ALONG THE WAY THANK YOU

TABLE OF CONTENTS

Sunrise

THE DAY AWAKENS
ENDLESS POSSIBILITIES
A NEW BEGINNING
A FRESH START

GRATITUDE FILLS ME
BLESSINGS ALL AROUND
WHICH STEP TO TAKE
WHICH DREAM TO CREATE

I CHOOSE GREATNESS
PURPOSE CANNOT BE IGNORED
SO MANY IN NEED
SO MANY TO INSPIRE

SEIZE EACH MOMENT
OUR TIME IS PRECIOUS
WE MUST REUNITE
WE MUST MOVE TOWARDS LOVE

THE DAY AWAKENS
ENDLESS POSSIBILITIES
OUR NEW BEGINNING
OUR FRESH START

I wrote that poem to be a tone setter for the reading of this book. Everyone is equally significant in the grand scheme. If you don't believe that now I hope you will by the end of your reading. Please Enjoy.

AUTHOR'S NOTE

I would like the reader to understand that this book is not intended to treat, cure, or prevent any physical or psychological disorder. The suggestions contained within the text are based upon the author's personal experience and results gained from taking these suggestions will vary. The author is not qualified to treat or diagnose, and any current medical or psychological disorders should be discussed with a licensed professional. The text within is intended to supplement any current lifestyle choices. The author's expertise lies within his life experience including 7 years of active substance addiction and 8 years of active recovery from substance addiction. No guarantees or promises can be made as to the effectiveness of statements made, although the author is confident that if implemented the reader should see positive changes. Please take or leave any of the statements made henceforth and determine for yourself the validity of each.

INTRODUCTION

The inspiration and first words of this book were born in February 2001. I was a junior in High School and had a sudden blast of motivation, the likes of which I did not know existed. I can remember a friend of mine saying, most likely jokingly, Caleb you should write a book. Well for some reason I took those words to heart and within a couple weeks I had left my school in an effort to write a book that would change the lives of all who read it.

I rode that wave of inspiration for 2 weeks, and at the end I had what I refer to as the first draft of this book. I came up with 10 chapters or lessons that I felt would lead the reader to a more fulfilling and successful life. I described each lesson as best I could at the age of 17, and at the end I was quite pleased with the work I had done. Needless to say, I had not yet acquired the life experience necessary to attempt writing something of this nature. Although

I do still feel that it was quite an accomplishment for me to write what I did at that time, I would quickly find out that I still had much to learn before I could teach.

What follows is my story from the time I returned to school after completing that first draft until the Spring of 2009. You will quickly see that even though my heart and intentions were in the right place I was clearly in no position to be offering up life altering advice to the masses. It is important for the reader to keep in mind that although my story is one of overcoming substance addiction, that is not a prerequisite for benefiting from the lessons laid out henceforth. I certainly hope that some who read this will be able to relate to my struggles and ideally use my experience to help overcome their own addictions. That being said, anyone who has not yet found their true calling in life and is in any way dissatisfied or confused by their current circumstance will profit from reading and implementing the lessons contained within this book.

After the reader has the chance to learn about my story and struggles it is time to reintroduce the 10 lessons in their new and improved form. Aside from a couple of minor word changes the titles of all 10 chapters remained the same over all those years. What did change was my life experiences and my ability to articulate the lessons in a much clearer and more usable way. I decided to add 3 exercises at the end of each chapter to allow the reader to fully incorporate the lessons into their day to day lives.

In Part 3 the individual will be given a recap of the lessons using examples from my life. I describe how I used those original principles to turn my life around from a place of confusion and hopelessness to that of purpose and joy. Hopefully this will enable the reader to further understand the lessons and apply them to their own life.

The book concludes with the original version of Chapter 1 exactly as it was written back in 2001. Although this addition is not critical to the overall message of the text I felt it was important to include at least a small portion of my original work. I decided to place this at the end of book to clearly show the reader how far my life has come since I was a 17 year old with dreams of helping the world.

I want to encourage the reader to fully utilize the text and exercises as they are described. If you are like me you will probably read through the entire book before stopping to do any of the suggested work. This is understandable, but in order to achieve the benefit and growth intended, I strongly suggest that after finishing the first time that the reader goes back and works on each lesson individually. Any book of this nature cannot be fully understood and applied to one's life without reading, re-reading, and taking the suggestions that are described within.

After more than a decade the intent for this book has never changed. I hope that it helps anyone who reads it to achieve a level of clarity and drive which enables them to live the life that they truly desire. Thank you for deciding to experience this long journey with me. Enjoy.

PART 1
STUMBLING OUT OF THE GATE

I am now sitting down again, after 7 years, to return to this project which started with such ferocity. The years since the conclusion of, "10 Steps on the Stairway to Heaven on Earth" have been long and winding. Throughout almost all of that time I strayed from the lessons upon which this book was founded. The whole experience started with a wave of confidence and energy unlike anything I had ever felt before. Even so my initial work has laid dormant over these past several years since that first wave crashed down upon the shoreline which was my life.

Fear, self-consciousness, anxiety, doubt, laziness, stagnation, and hesitation all played roles in keeping me from pursuing this goal which was the original intention from the start of this project. All the things about which I have spoken and described as enemies to human growth came together in my own life to hinder me from moving forward with my dream that I was once so passionate about. I am not proud of the fact that it has taken me so long to re-ignite this flame, but I know that my life unfolded the way it did for good reason.

Existence for me became funny, then reckless, followed by purposelessness, and ultimately very sad and seemingly hopeless. With the help of many people and some honest soul searching I have been able to get to the other side of it, but I found out first-hand how dangerous it is to not practice what you preach. I had life figured out at the age of 17, or so I thought, but it quickly became apparent that I was not yet at the end of my spiritual journey.

The pages that follow will describe the significant events which took place for me up to the point where I restored my focus and energy to the complete this book. When I finished the first 10 chapters I felt like I was on top of the world. I was filled with a confidence and an inner peace which I never realized existed. I was completely sure that I was going to pursue the publication of my work and millions of people searching for answers in life would benefit from it. Since I had only missed 2 weeks of school while writing those first chapters, I decided with the encouragement of some close friends to return to high school with the intention of continuing to move towards my goal of being published.

As it turned out, this was the beginning of the end of my new found confidence and determination. I had devoted the previous weeks to putting my beliefs and experiences on how I felt life should be lived onto paper, but almost immediately following my return to campus something inside me shifted. I expected to receive a warm welcome, but the reality which unfolded was much different. Rather than a majority of my peers being impressed by the work I had done, most met me with ridicule and doubt. My true friends remained, but outside of the close few I was labeled as crazy and the hard work I had put in was dismissed unseen.

This happened within a very short period of time, and the project which had brought me such a sense of accomplishment was diminished to a sense of shame just as quickly. From that point until at least 2 years later I cringed at the mention of this book. All the things that I had written about which would have told me to ignore the doubts of both myself and others and continue towards my dreams were lost and I was left feeling very confused and empty. It is amazing looking back on those few days to see what a profound impact they had on the rest of my life.

As I mentioned, upon completing the first 10 chapters I was at a high point of my relatively short life prior to returning to school and being met with that unexpected reception. From that initial high I was thrown into an overwhelming downward spiral which landed me at a critical and debilitating low. Fear, doubt, self-hatred, confusion, and self-consciousness, came into my psyche so powerfully that I was left feeling as a shell of the person I had once been so proud of. I was in no way prepared for this sudden reversal of perspective.

During the weeks leading up to the start of this book until its conclusion I was actually living in the way that I hoped all who read the book would live. I had such clarity and purpose that I assumed that what I was feeling would never go away. Now that my reality had been turned upside down so abruptly I had no idea what I was supposed to be doing next. All my plans of spreading my message in order to aid humankind were reduced to near oblivion. This, I feel, was a turning point which led me down the path that I chose next and ultimately back to a place where I could finish this text which I started so many years ago.

During my initial writing I briefly mentioned the use of drugs and my belief that if used purely for enjoyment and not in order to cover up any sort of dissatisfaction that it was acceptable or even beneficial for some. Up until that time in my life I had used drugs recreationally without any substantial consequences. By my standards I had not altered my consciousness in order to escape any significant inner turmoil. This fact changed when I returned to drugs not only for recreation but to allow me to forget the shame and remorse of having my dreams extinguished so suddenly. I had passed the point of no return.

At the time I was certainly not aware of it, but from then on I used drugs and alcohol in a way that I could no longer justify as mere choice. My life from then on unfolded into a series of events which eventually lead me to another crossroads and back to the path I always intended to walk.

Now that my world had been changed so dramatically I no longer felt comfortable being around most of the people who up until then I had called my friends. I did not lose everyone, but in many instances I became overwhelmed by my insecurities in situations which had previously been routine and enjoyable. I found it very difficult to communicate with my peers because I second guessed everything that was about to come out of my mouth. I went from being a person who gained energy and happiness from being around people to someone who was drained by and terrified of the thought of social situations. For several months after I returned to school I isolated myself to a greater degree than I ever had before; for me getting high was the only occasional relief I got from what I was feeling.

At this same time the people who I used to hang out with stopped calling or making any effort to be around me. This of course gave me further reason to continue my isolation and feel more shame about the work I had done. It was a constant struggle to get through a school day where I had to see all of the people who I could no longer look in the eyes. I felt my skin crawling at all times and I had no idea how to get out of the rut I was in. Looking back it is truly amazing how quickly I forgot all that I had been so passionate about just days or weeks before. I also realize now that all the people who I thought had turned on me stopped thinking about what I had done more quickly than I did.

As is most often the case, all of my misery and emotional turbulence were of my own making. Had I decided that I was not going to allow the opinion of a few people to control me so thoroughly, my reality at that time would have been much different. Instead I chose to exaggerate the events in my head and lose my drive towards success and helping people. All this was taking place during the second half of my junior year in high school.

Unable to function socially because of what I imagined people were saying about me, I spent most of those months either alone or with my lifelong friend who lived in my neighborhood. My life during that period of time consisted of me being asleep on the couch, trying to fall asleep, or getting high and or drunk. I truly was in such pain that I never wanted to just be in my reality. It was a very sad way to live, but at the time I really did not see any alternatives. I can't remember experiencing a genuine smile or laughter at all during those months. I found pleasure in nothing and only slight comfort in my ability to alter my consciousness.

Some of my friends and family were concerned about the sudden change in me. I am sure they wanted to help me, but I also know that I was intended to experience all of it. Even though I had the solution to my agonizing state of being that whole time, today I can be grateful that I went through it. It now gives me even more motivation to not be in that place again and to live a healthy, happy, and productive life. This initial period of drug abuse, isolation, depression, and self-hate continued on for about 6 months until I was given a wonderful opportunity by my parents.

The gift offered me a chance to escape the pattern that I was in. It was a 3 week Outward Bound wilderness experience, and it came at a time when I had really nothing at all to look forward to each day. The trip was planned for the end of my summer vacation just prior to my senior year. Although the thought of it did initiate quite a bit of fear and apprehension, I was hopeful that the experience would help to bring me out of the perpetual darkness I was feeling.

So after months of drug abuse and self-pity, I left for North Carolina in search of myself again. I didn't know what I was getting myself into but I knew that it could not make me feel any worse than I already did. Unfortunately it turned out that I was even wrong about that. When I got off the plane to meet with the people I would be spending the next 3 weeks with, the reality that I would be forced to interact with strangers 24/7 without the use of drugs or alcohol hit me with a jolt.

Everyone else seemed to be relatively happy and comfortable, aside from me who felt as if I was in one of those dreams where you go to school naked. I felt so self-conscious and awkward that I was barely able to make small talk with a couple of the other group members. All the other people were about my age and were not intimidating in any way. The problem was my vulnerability and my complete lack of self-confidence and self-worth. As soon as I was in that environment and felt the way I felt, I regretted having decided to go on that trip. I had no idea how I was going to make it through that first day, let alone the entire 3 weeks.

As I described earlier, my social anxiety was almost unbearable at the start of our excursion. Everyone else seemed to easily adapt and socialize with each other while I struggled to even join in any of the conversations. I was so overwhelmed by fear and doubt that I could only manage the briefest and simplest of interactions. At night most of the others would stay up and tell stories about themselves, and even though I had had similar experiences, I dreaded the thought of having to talk in front of this group. (All of 10 people my own age)

Somehow despite my mental and emotional discomfort I was able to push through it. Outward Bound trips are extremely demanding physically and slowly I did start to feel a little bit better. Most days consisted of either hiking or canoeing from sun up to sundown and I am certain that the high level of activity helped to get my mind and body back in balance.

After about 2 weeks I felt like I was almost back to my old self again. I had lengthy conversations with my group members and laughed and joked as I hadn't in months. It turned out that pretty much the only thing I had in common with these people was an affinity for getting high, so most of the conversations involved glorification or exaggeration of my drug use. I remember being asked why I didn't talk for most of the trip and I managed to just avoid the question. It did not even cross my mind that I had been sober this entire time and that that might have been partly responsible for my renewed state of mind.

I returned home happy that the trip was over and eager to get back to my previous lifestyle. Some part of me knew that exercise and abstaining from partying was of benefit to me, but as soon as I was home the thought did not reach my conscious mind.

I returned home feeling better than I had in many months and immediately made a call so that I could get high. Again I was simply not able to make the connection between a healthy lifestyle and my emotional wellbeing at that time. I spent the rest of my summer working part time and getting wasted the rest. All in all I was just glad to not be in the same state I had been in the 6 months prior.

The summer came to an end quickly and I was back in school for my final year. I was not excited about starting another school year but I was not dreading it either. The year started off smoothly mainly because I only had 3 classes and they were all electives. My day was manageable and it was apparent that everything that had transpired at the end of my junior year had been forgotten. It was business as usual, and I was happy to coast through school and get high all afternoon.

After only about a week of this I decided to skip my first two periods and sleep in. A friend of mine called me that morning looking for a ride and agreed to come in late with me. She had some weed to smoke on the ride in. I was not opposed to the idea so I picked her up and we did just that.

I arrived at school in good spirits and took my seat in my third period class. Not 10 minutes later my name was being called over the PA system to go directly to the dean's office. Needless to say I sobered up very quickly. When I arrived, the dean, school nurse, security guard and police officer were all waiting for me. I acted as calmly as I could and did what they asked of me. I was evaluated by the school nurse who reported that I did not appear to be under the influence of any substances, and I did not have anything illegal on my person.

When I came out from my evaluation I asked if I could go; thinking that I had dodged a bullet. I was very displeased to find out that my car had already been searched and paraphernalia was found. At that point I knew I was in trouble and could only wait and see what was going to happen. Shortly after I was being handcuffed and escorted down to the police station on charges of drug paraphernalia on school grounds.

For a long time this event was a source of pride for me rather than an indication that my drug use was becoming a problem in my life. It was the first of many significant consequences and it amazes me that I took it so lightly at the time. My "consequence" from school was an extra 2 weeks of summer vacation (aka a suspension) and until much later on I did not have a negative thought about the ordeal.

From that point on my whole attitude on life seemed to change radically. Up until then I had been a respectful kid and generally cared about the feelings of others. After coming back from my school suspension my mission in life was to question any authority figure and do my best to hurt anyone who stood between me and whatever I wanted to do. I was not physically violent towards anyone but for the next several years I emotionally abused all the people in my life that really cared about me and wanted to see me happy. Part of this can be attributed to normal teenage rebellion, but in my opinion it was largely due to the fact that drugs had taken my ability to look at my actions and choices in a realistic light.

I did not lose many friendships at that time; the primary damage I did was to my immediate family. In my eyes what I was doing was perfectly normal because I chose to surround myself with people who partied to the same extent that I did. Although this was true, I am confident that the majority of those friends were able to move on with their lives after high school. As the school year progressed my interest in anything outside of getting messed up and hanging out quickly diminished. I did the minimum amount of work needed to get decent grades and one of my first loves in life, which was sports, lost all importance to me.

I certainly did not recognize it at the time but it was clear to an outsider that my life was totally ruled by mind altering substances by the age of 17. Getting high took precedence over anything else which had previously been relevant to me. It is strange to admit with some clarity of mind today, but it was certainly impossible for me to admit it to myself at that time.

My senior year of high school was not particularly eventful after that run in with the law. The most significant aspect of it was the fact that I was living alone with my dad the entire year. This was because my mom had taken a job on Martha's Vineyard which is where we were moving upon my graduation. That year with my dad was significant because it so clearly illustrated the deterioration that had occurred within my heart and soul.

Growing up my Dad had been a constant role model for me. He embodied what it meant to work hard and provide for a family, and I never went without anything my entire life. He is and was a spiritual seeker and much of my beliefs today stemmed from him and the impression he made on me from a young age. Although it is natural for children to stray from their parents during high school I believe that the way I treated my father was due to the change that had occurred in me since drugs had taken over my life.

I knew from a very young age that my dad had also gone through a struggle with every day drug use even though I have no recollection of him ever being high or drunk around me. He quit when I was 3 years old as a result of my mom threatening to leave him. I knew that it was very painful for him to watch me go down the same path which had caused so many problems for him in the past. This knowledge did not make me hesitate or alter my behavior in the least. It was almost as if I consciously kept throwing it in his face even while seeing how much it hurt him. During that year we lived together as strangers. We did not talk except to dismiss each other or argue about some trivial house issue. I treated my dad as if he had been my enemy since birth, when the reality was all he had ever done was love and guide me all those years. Somehow my perception of him had changed from seeing him as a great man who was always there for me to some random person who stood in the way of me and my selfish desires.

Even now it is hard for me to reflect on this period because I now have a realistic picture of the person I had become. It is amazing to me how blind I was to the damage that I caused to everyone around me. All of the positive traits which my parents instilled in me during my childhood had been transformed into my single minded purpose of getting high and staying high.

Although I had not put any significant effort towards school since before I started high school, I was accepted to my first choice school, the University of Maine, on early admissions. This happened only half way through my senior year so along with being exciting it also just gave me further reason to not really care about anything besides having fun and hanging out. At that time I did not think about or have any idea of the level of commitment that it took to pursue and complete a college education. I basically only applied because everyone else did and I had always planned on it.

My final year of high school went by in a blur. I missed the maximum amount of days in every class and did as little work as I possibly could. I was essentially numb to the world, and was not aware that I had lost my purpose in life. Days and weeks just ran together and all I was capable of was being physically present at school and getting high all other waking hours. Somehow I was in a mind state where that not only felt acceptable but also normal.

When I first used drugs I was very concerned that they would change my mind and spirit and it happened so gradually that I was not aware of it. Life was pretty much a big joke; and I allowed it to unfold that way not realizing that I was the punch line. If anyone tried to mention that my life was out of control I either denied it, defended it, or dismissed it completely. Little did I know that that entire defense was not really me anymore, but rather an addiction to chemicals to get me through my days.

Like I said earlier I was accepted into the University of Maine midway through my senior year. The plan for my parents had long been to move to Martha's Vineyard at the end of the summer before I went to college. I had somehow blocked that out of my consciousness and had gone along as if my life was not going to change at all. I did not really come to terms with how serious a move it was going to be to start college and come home to a place where I had never lived.

Nevertheless I pushed those thoughts out of my mind and continued with summer behaving in the same reckless manner. I didn't have the motivation to have a job even while knowing that I was going to have to use my own money for everything besides food while I was at school. I was truly a shell of a person and my only reason for getting up each morning was the prospect of getting high that day. I lost touch with most of the people I had gone to school with aside from a couple lifelong friends who lived in my neighborhood. It felt like anything besides finding and using drugs and alcohol was too much for me to handle.

The end of summer came without warning and before I knew it I was packing up the house in which I had spent my entire cognitive life. I still had no concept of the reality that I was about to begin. I was going into college without any preparation or knowledge of how to work hard and study in school. On top of that I was leaving the only place that I had any significant memory of living, and where all of my friends still resided. On some level I knew that I was not capable of drinking and using drugs to the extent that I had been if I had any hope of being successful in college. I remember thinking that I would be able to start fresh and meet people who did not need drugs or alcohol to have fun.

A week prior to the start of my college career my parents and I left my home town for Martha's Vineyard. The expectation was that I was moving on with my life and they were starting the next chapter of their lives together in the place they had long dreamed of living. Although the plan started off as expected, it did not take long for me and my careless lifestyle to alter everything.

I had done nothing to prepare myself for the adjustment necessary to be successful in college. Nevertheless I was oddly confident that things would work out and suddenly I could return to being a person capable of hard work and dedication to academic goals. I was a little nervous to be in a new environment, but mostly just excited for the opportunity I was being given.

In a flash I was unpacked and my parents were on their way back to their new life. As I mentioned earlier I had no real plan of continuing on with my drinking and drug use and did have a real desire to do well in school which at one point in my life had been a priority. Even with all these hopes and resolutions I found myself buying drugs and getting to know a dealer within a couple of hours of arriving in my dorm. It has since become clear to me that this happened against my will due to the fact that I had lost the ability to socialize and relate to people without the use of mind altering substances. It did not seem significant at the time but hindsight has enabled me to see that this simple choice revealed a much deeper malady which I could not admit I was experiencing.

From that first night, academia took a backseat to meeting new people and partying to excess. As is always the case I very quickly fell in with the crowd who were more interested in where the party was than where their next class was. I was only able to hold it together for about a month at which point I stopped attending any of my classes at all. It is astonishing to me now to realize that this completely reckless and irresponsible lifestyle did not alarm me in the least at the time. I was able to divorce myself from reality in the midst of the people I was with who were largely doing the very same things.

Aside from a couple of memorable events my college experience was a blur. Each day was the same as the previous in which I woke up and immediately started my mission of drinking and getting high that day. I told myself that I was having a great time and at times I can honestly say I was, but for the most part I was losing myself in the obsession to get "fucked up." My overwhelming need to get high became even more apparent once I ran out of money. At that point I resorted to selling almost everything in my dorm room for a fraction of what it was worth. Again this was not of concern to me while it was happening.

Finally after about 2 and half months of this constant drug finding endeavor, it dawned on me that I had written a book and that all of my money problems would be solved if I pursued its publication. I immediately made a call to my parents and let them in on my master plan. I informed them that it would be a waste for me to stay at school and that I did not want to cost them anymore money. This plan occurred to me after about a month of sleeping only about 2-3 hours a night and constantly being intoxicated to an extent I never had been before. Needless to say my parents were a little troubled by the phone call and arrived at my school several days earlier than I expected. My college career which had started with much potential and enthusiasm was over before I had completed even one semester.

My parents met me with open arms and I left the University of Maine with only a couple of phone numbers and memories to show for it. In addition I had developed, as doctors put it, an overactive brain which had been ignited by lack of sleep and habitual drug and alcohol abuse. I thought that my mind was the clearest it had ever been, but apparently my parents did not agree and shortly after I was admitted to a psychiatric ward for the first of several extended visits. This experience was another significant turning point for me which lead to a drawn out period of misery and hopelessness

Ironically I was drugged prior to entering the facility because I was so wound up, and when I came to and realized where I was and why I was there I was not a happy camper. Again I felt as though I was thinking and feeling better than I ever had before, so to be in a place like this was not welcomed. It soon became clear to me that I would not be able to leave this facility until I agreed to take medication for the problem the doctors inaccurately diagnosed. Reluctantly I agreed in part due to the fact that I was in a ward with other young people who also seemed to be relatively normal like me. I remained there for about a week and was discharged. I believe this was in large part due to the fact that I was a huge pain in the ass to all of the doctors and psychiatrists in the facility that I met.

I left this hospital a little less energetic and a lot angrier. I felt betrayed by my parents who had sent me there even though I had plans to publish my book and live happily ever after. I could not believe that they would treat their only son like this, and now I was forced to move back in with them in a place I had visited but in which I had never lived.

It took me only a few days to realize that I was far from all my friends and more importantly had no way of obtaining drugs and alcohol. A month prior I was still on course to get a 4 year degree and move forward in my life. Now I was stuck living at home again with zero social network. In no time all the excitement and motivation I had left school with vanished and morphed into almost unbearable insecurities and depression. Once again I would face an uphill battle to change my bleak outlook on life.

The first thing I managed to do was get a job. It actually suited me well for a little while since I didn't really have to think or have any long inter-actions with other people. Also I worked 6 days a week which was good in the sense that it occupied my time and distracted me from how I was feeling. The problem was when I was not there or had time to stop and think, all I could feel was my intense desire to have friendships/drug connections. I was completely sober throughout that time for the longest continuous period since I began high school. I saw no benefit to this, and was very uncomfortable the whole time unless I was asleep. I didn't realize it then but my life had become so centered on getting high that it had become almost unbearable to live without it.

This mental and emotional discomfort continued for a couple of months. I was working all the time and making decent money considering my age and skill set. In turn I was allowed to save more money than I ever had before. I felt terrible most of the time but it was nice to be able to put some money in the bank for once.

As I mentioned earlier, one of the few things that I had gained from college was a few phone numbers. One of those phone numbers happened to be from someone who grew up on Martha's Vineyard. As soon as I knew she would be back from winter break I gave her a call. As a result of that call I was invited to a New Year's Eve party a couple days later. I finally relaxed a little bit and had something to look forward to for the first time in a while. My mood elevated for the first time since leaving the hospital and only because I knew I would have the opportunity to get high and drunk again. That alone made it much easier to get through the next couple of days.

I made it through a few more days of work and arrived at the party without really knowing any-one, but eager to get some chemicals in my body. In no time I was sent back into that false sense of wellbeing which I had relied upon so heavily over the past several years. After that first hit and sip nothing else seemed to matter and I could take a deep breath at last. I was changed in that moment and my desire to maintain this state of mind returned with full force.

I was not able to go back to daily intoxication right after that night, but my mind was clearly set on achieving that goal. In my short time at my job I had become a reliable and trusted worker while not drinking or doing drugs. Soon after my night of partying my restlessness with the job intensified greatly and I started to think that it was the source of my dissatisfaction with life. I somehow got it in my head that I needed to move back to Connecticut and re-unite with my friends. I had no realistic way of doing this but nevertheless I planned a trip back. At the same time I put in my two weeks' notice because in my mind I was going to figure something out when I got there. Keep in mind that these thoughts of quitting my job and moving to Connecticut had not been present prior to me altering my consciousness and I had only done that the one time.

Since I had no living expenses my working had allowed me to save a good chunk of money. This savings was spent wisely on a large quantity of pot just before I left for my visit/attempt at moving. I would be staying with my best friend and my hope was to find a job and new place to live in 2 or 3 days.

I do not remember much from that trip, all I know is that I had gone there with more money than I ever had, and I returned having accomplished none of the things I hoped to do and with no money left to show for it. This was one of many clear examples of how drugs and alcohol contributed to me losing my ability to think or act rationally and make wise decisions. I threw away a good job with potential for growth because my desire to get high and relive the past eliminated my sense of reality concerning my actions.

Upon returning from my 72 hour escapade I felt much worse than when I left. I was broke, jobless, living with my parents, had no friends in sight, and realized that I would not be able to go back to my former life which I valued so much. Once again I was stuck without any way to change the way I was feeling or even distract myself from it. I felt hopeless and empty. Even though I was not physically able to get high or drink my mind was constantly consumed by thoughts of how I was going to do those things again. It truly was one of the darkest points in my drinking and drug-using history.

This went on for a few months until the weather started to change and some of the seasonal businesses of Martha's Vineyard started to open. This meant an opportunity for a new job and possibly some reliable ways of getting drugs. Martha's Vineyard attracts people from all over the country during the summer months and many of them get temporary work when it is needed in those peak weeks. Fortunately for me the majority of those people were young and more interested in partying than whatever company they happened to be working for.

I easily found work because I was already there and most other employees would not arrive for another month or two. Again I became liked at my job and worked hard during the time that I was not getting wasted. Being around people again made me feel a little better at times but underneath that was the growing need to get "fucked up" again.

Soon enough my ticket to emotional detachment arrived. Luckily for me he had been working at the business for a couple of years and already knew many people who could help me relieve my anxiety. Almost overnight I was partying like I had prior to moving, and for me all was right with the world. I was hanging out with older people so getting alcohol was not a problem and since the summer crowd was there I had access to other methods of intoxication as well.

Little did I know that although I was finally feeling like my old self my bosses were not sharing in my sentiment. Apparently I was not quite as dependable anymore and within only a few weeks I went from being valued and well liked to getting fired. Of course I blamed it all on my boss being an asshole, but in retrospect my drug problem certainly did take away any motivation or initiative that I had shown previously.

That summer saw me in constant pursuit of an altered state of mind and although I was able to stay employed after that point, I most definitely did not return to being any sort of model worker. I became friends with a couple more people who did not seem to think that my behavior was abnormal. Again my life turned into Groundhog Day where I worked during the day and got as messed up as possible at night. The startling fact was that even though I was able to party like I wanted to it was becoming much harder to shake off the feelings of loneliness and lack of self-worth. Drinking and getting high was beginning to fail me at its one job of making me feel better.

Again this was an alarming realization because mind altering substances had been my only defense against complete demoralization. If they didn't work anymore I didn't know what I was going to do. Coincidentally right about the same time my parents were noticing that I was having a very hard time coping with life. In response to this they started to research possible solutions that would relieve me of some of the pain that I was obviously going through. Once again Outward Bound was brought to my attention. They had found an 81 day semester program that was offered and I was presented with the idea. I was very reluctant at first, thinking that I would be separated from my ability to get high for that long, but I did not dismiss it completely.

As the days passed it became clear that I needed drastic action in order to jump start my life again. I soon made the decision to go through with the Outward Bound idea. In my mind going on that trip would give me an opportunity to clear out the fog for a while and meet some people that I could relate to and build friendships with. Although my parents expected this trip to end my drinking and drug using career, I was not on the same page as they.

The decision to go to that semester did not change my behavior at all. Even though I knew how physically demanding the experience was going to be, I did almost nothing to get in better shape before I left. I continued to abuse my body daily with drugs and alcohol and did little to no physical exercise. I was essentially able to push the thought of going out of my consciousness because I knew it would be hard and I didn't want to think about it.

I don't know how long it was in between my decision and when I left, but soon enough the day came to depart. I was heading out to Utah in hopes of finding some good friends and some peace of mind. I had no idea that I would find that and much more.

In spite of the fact that I did not intend to quit drinking and doing drugs after I came back from the trip, I did expect to avoid getting high while I was there. For whatever reason that did not end up being the case. Within an hour or two of arriving at my hotel, I met the two people who would become my close friends. As it happened one of them had already come across some weed so even before my first day was over my intentions of sobriety were dismissed.

From that first meeting forward I had a very strong bond with these two people. I was also delighted to find out the next day that out of the three separate groups going out they were both in same one as me. We all headed out into the wilderness of Utah the next day and very shortly afterward I realized that I should have done at least some physical preparation. We started at about 8,000 feet elevation as opposed to sea level which I had lived in my entire life. My body did not appreciate this drastic change in elevation and level of exertion so within the first couple miles of hiking I was vomiting up my breakfast. The altitude sickness would subside after a few days, but it was yet another indication of how drugs and alcohol had taken priority over my physical wellbeing.

The trip also started similarly to my other Outward Bound in that I felt very insecure and withdrawn in the beginning. Aside from those two people I made friends with on the first night, I was very uncomfortable talking to anyone. Overall though, I was glad that I made the choice to come and saw that my goals for going could be met.

After the initial altitude sickness I had no other physical problems for the rest of the trip. Somehow though, I was faced once again with an opportunity to get high only a week into our hiking. One of those friends in my group found a bag of weed that had been dropped on the trail. In our minds The Universe was clearly telling us that we should take advantage of this unlikely circumstance. My intention to abstain from drugs and alcohol was proving to be much harder than expected. Luckily that first drug escapade went off without any consequence. It would later prove to be a hindrance to our judgment.

The adventure continued as planned, and although I remained fairly withdrawn from most of my group I was beginning to feel better internally. The combination of physical exertion and sobriety was lifting my spirits as I hoped it would. Unfortunately for me and my two partners in crime, this course did not keep us in the wilderness from start to finish. Due to the length of it there were two scheduled rest periods at hotels within civilization.

These short breaks would prove to be much less beneficial than they were intended to be. In fact they provided ample opportunity to further derail my ability to avoid mind altering substances and hopes of getting a clearer perspective on my life. That first pit stop was the beginning of the end of my vow to maintain physical sobriety on the trip.

I managed to stay intoxicated almost the entire time and completely wasted the opportunity to let my body rest. In fact I was sleep deprived by the end of the two days and went back out in worse shape than I came in. Again I didn't think of it then, but it was another glaring example of how being under the influence took precedence over everything else in my life.

To make a long story short, all the friends that I made on the trip and I got kicked out for bringing weed out on course. It is truly amazing to me now how indifferent I felt about that happening when it did. I was even able to convince myself that it was the fault of the people who told the counselors. I threw away a significant amount of money and a huge opportunity to help myself and felt almost no remorse over it. All I could focus on was the fact that I would have the chance to go back to doing exactly what I had been doing before.

I won't say that the trip was a total loss because I did make two lasting friends with whom I remain in close touch. The reality is though, that I chose to get high rather than take an objective look at my life while I had the chance. It still astonishes me how emotionally shut off I became due to drinking and drug abuse, along with the fact that I had no regard for anything besides my selfish motives anymore. Almost exactly a year after I had abruptly and prematurely left college, I was now doing the same from Outward Bound.

Needless to say my family was disappointed and disheartened by the reality that I could not manage to stay sober for even that relatively short period of time. I don't know how badly my parents were hurt by my expulsion from the program, but I do know that I didn't feel badly about it at all. As I said earlier I could not internalize the pain that I caused others. In my mind all that mattered was that I could party every day again. My parents figured that this event would be enough to show me that my actions were not working anymore, but somehow I was not yet convinced. When I told them that I had no plans of stopping they informed me that I would no longer be allowed to live with them.

For me this was only a minor bump in the road and I quickly moved in with two of my friends. There is no point in detailing anymore of my reckless behavior after that time. I had become a person whose sole purpose was to find ways to get and stay high. I did not turn into a monster in the sense of violence or crime, but I did lose what was left of my identity, integrity and self-worth. My parents and other family never stopped caring and trying to help me. The problem was that I stopped caring about myself and therefore did not see a need for help. The drugs and alcohol allowed me to believe that I was having a good time and leading a meaningful life, but the opposite was true.

For about the next two years all I could manage to do was go to work at some mindless job which paid me just enough to keep my habit going. I did not even realize that the kindhearted and moti-vated person I had once been no longer existed in my day to day life. My constant intoxication led me to 3 more arrests and hospitalizations over that 2 year span. Even so I did not recognize myself as having a problem until the very end. I always could place the blame on bad luck or just not being care-ful enough; never that I needed to stop this lifestyle altogether.

Then, for no reason in particular in the fall of 2005 I had had enough. This time did not mark a point of intolerable depression or any traumatic event. For whatever reason, I was then able to let my guard down and accepted the help my parents had been offering for so long. After discussing it with a family psychiatrist, I agreed to go into residential drug and alcohol treatment. I was in no way excited about my decision, but thankfully I was given enough clarity to go through with it.

I made the choice to go into rehab at the beginning of September. My admittance date was not until the end of the month so of course I got in as much partying as I could in that period of time. At the end I can honestly say that I got no enjoyment out of the use of drugs and alcohol, but nevertheless could not stop. To me the non-enjoyment I felt while intoxicated was at least a little better than the way I felt the rest of the time.

As was my habit I tried not to think about the reality of what I was about to do, knowing that it would not be easy. Until I boarded the plane for rehab I managed to forget that that was my destination. It hadn't hit me yet that I was making a decision that would dramatically alter the course of my life. All I knew was that I had to make it through 28 days at this place without getting high. I felt scared, timid, reluctant, anxious, and just a little hopeful as I had on the plane to my previous Outward Bound expedition. I had no idea then that I was starting a journey that would end up being more difficult and rewarding than any other before it. I cannot say that my first day of rehab was my first day of continuous sobriety, but nonetheless my journey had begun.

Much like all the other attempts I had in trying to turn my life around, it began awkwardly. I entered the facility to find about 20 guys around my age who seemed to be comfortable with each other and having a good time. I became very aware of the fact that I was sober and had no way of changing that. Most of the people there had relatively strong personalities and although they were friendly and welcoming, I did not feel at ease right away. Immediately I was counting down the minutes to my discharge.

I met some people and saw my room along with a couple of other guys who had arrived with me. Thus began my first day of treatment. I don't remember much about that day aside from the feelings of insecurity and self-consciousness. Nevertheless I managed to make it through the first week and began to feel more comfortable. Our days were occupied with groups, therapy, meals and speakers at night. It wasn't bad and I quickly learned how to act and what to say to please the staff. By the end of 2 weeks I had made some rehab friends and was having a decent time without drugs for the first time in several years. I had gotten a chance to look at the extent to which my drinking and drug abuse had reached. I wrote down my whole history along with all the damage that my behavior had caused others around me. It was the first time I had ever truly taken an honest look at those years of my life and it was eye-opening seeing it all there in front of me.

At this same time my parents came to visit. I felt pretty good about myself and I was able to be honest with them about things I had done and apologize for how I had mistreated them over the years. This simple act refers to the first chapter of this book because it allowed me to be honest after years of feeling like I had to lie. I can say that it was liberating and it did a great deal in starting the healing process between me and my parents. Unfortunately I can't say that this initial good experience with honesty was enough to keep me away from drugs or lying. Shortly after that visit I was offered the chance to smoke some weed and I took it. Now here again the insanity of drug addiction shows its face. I was in treatment voluntarily to stop doing drugs, I was feeling better than I had in a long time, and I risked losing that along with the progress I had made with my family. I did not have any prior desire to get high but when given the chance I didn't say no. Clearly the choice of whether or not I should get high was not mine anymore. I had no reason to smoke that weed and all the reasons in the world not to and I did it anyway. This was insanity to anyone rational who would have seen it, but completely normal to me at the time.

What that one incident did for me was allow me to believe again that I could get high without consequence. I did not get caught and of course the rest of my stay there was wasted because it revolved around a lie. I didn't give myself a chance to be free of my obsession, so I left that program for another under the false premise that I had been sober the whole time.

From the moment I got to the next program, I was forced to lie to everyone there and my whole family. Under these circumstances I again gave myself no shot at accomplishing my goal of stopping the use of drugs and alcohol for good. I was able to say the right things to make everyone believe the lie I was living, while at the same time I was convincing myself that I could go back to partying and be fine.

It is crazy to think how warped my thought process had become and how easily I was able to be dishonest. The result of my irrational thinking and dishonest behavior was that I started finding ways to get high while I was still in treatment. I figured out how to get cough medicine which can be used as a hallucinogen in high doses and was abusing prescribed medication. I can now look back and see that dishonesty and my obsession to alter my consciousness were directly related. I had lied so long about what I was doing that the two actions fueled each other.

All the behind the scenes bullshit that I was doing ultimately led to the culmination of my drinking and drug using career to this day. I was nearing the end of my stay in residential treatment after close to 90 days combined in the 2 facilities. It was mid-December and the rehab I was in had their annual Christmas party for residents and alumni of the program. This party allowed the male and female clients to have extended interaction which was not permitted on a normal day. In short, I and two other participants of the program came up with a plan to sneak out that night and get drunk.

Seeing as how I had been getting high and lying about it consistently for my entire stay this plan sounded pretty solid to me. Never did it cross my mind that my purpose for being there was solely to help solve my problem with drugs and alcohol. It didn't occur to me either that these other two people were there for the same reason and we all had families that would be devastated by our actions. As I've said my motives were purely selfish at that time and I was incapable of looking beyond any possible immediate benefit to me.

In short, the plan went off without a hitch and the three of us ventured out onto the streets of Long Beach. I did not know it then but this would be my last event of this nature. It started out with my thinking that we would buy alcohol, get drunk and have some fun. The reality as usual was much different. Walking back from the liquor store we were approached with a proposition to smoke some speed which sounded logical in the moment.

One of us was not interested so we left her with the alcohol and promised to return in 30 minutes. Thus began a 4 hour drug induced late night tour of Long Beach. We never did meet back up with that girl and luckily aside from a couple bruises from falling down drunk, she made it back safely to our rehab. Again I acted with extreme self-centered insanity.

Before that night was over smoking speed turned into weed that turned into cocaine. I remember feeling at the time that what I was doing was crazy, but I had no will to stop myself. That was the last time that I ingested any mind altering substance, and the only reason I stopped then was because my counterpart that night confessed to everything we did in the morning. It is very possible that if she hadn't I would still be in the same state I was in or worse because I had no intention of telling anyone.

Needless to say I was not welcome to stay at that facility any longer and I ended up in the program which gave me my life back. Thankfully for me it was and hopefully will be the last program I ever have to attend. Fortunately I had finally reached the point where I could no longer convince myself that I was capable of getting high and living a meaningful life.

After about a week staying in a detox center I was presented with an opportunity to go to a recovery house in Los Angeles. I was told that I would stay for 3 months and after a short time I would get a job and get my life going again. I agreed to go mainly because I had no money and I was 3000 miles away from my family who wouldn't have taken me in anyway. It didn't sound too bad and 3 months was a manageable timeframe to deal with.

Although none of the initial things I was told turned out to be true, I am extremely grateful that I had enough willingness to at least agree to move in. The place was called the Miracle House and it was a large home in the Miracle Mile district of LA. As soon as I got there I noticed that this place was like nothing I had ever been a part of. The house consisted of two managers who lived on site and about 15 guys who were mostly all about my age. The difference that I noticed right off the bat was that these guys were sober and able to exist comfortably and have fun anyway. All the other hospitals and programs I had been in had people that were basically serving time until their next high. Here everyone seemed dedicated to staying sober and improving themselves. I have to admit that it was a little overwhelming while at the same time comforting.

As is my custom I did not immediately become socially confident. I talked to people a little bit but mostly observed what was going on and took it in. The majority of the guys there were welcoming and cool to hang out with, so it didn't take long for me to adapt and settle in. I also learned the rules and the message the house was trying to convey within my first month.

The message was to be honest and take responsibility for your actions. Although I knew these things were the key to a happy and productive life, it was not easy living that way again after so many years of lying to myself and others. I had forgotten what it was like to admit when I was wrong and the freedom that came from telling the truth. For the first time in my life my friends and peers were not allowing me to go against these basic guidelines for living. You got caught in a lie or else your conscience got the best of you and you told the truth on your own.

As I mentioned I went into the house thinking that I would be there for 3 months and soon start working and getting my life back on track. I ended up staying the entire 1 year of the program because it was the only time since I had become addicted to drugs that allowed me to do the right thing and not need to chemically alter the way that I felt. Again it all came back to being honest. Now that I had nothing to hide, the feelings of guilt and inadequacy which in part caused me to excessively use drugs and alcohol were gone. The solution which I knew and had written about 5 years prior worked for me once again.

Since the first day that I was able to be true to myself and others I have not found it necessary to change the way I feel through any kind of drug. It amazes me now that although I was aware of this fact, I was unable to let it work when the drugs and opportunity were all around me. I never thought that anything could take away my ability to make my own decisions or think rationally. As long as I lived that lie and stayed under the influence I thought I was making my own decisions, but really the drugs were doing it for me.

The year that I lived in the Miracle House went by in a flash and I actually have very few distinct memories from that time period. What I do know is that as time passed I became more and more comfortable being myself. The illusion that drugs and alcohol were the source of any fun and excitement in my life slowly went away. I remembered that prior to the addiction setting in I found joy and excitement in many activities and I was now free to find those things again.

When it was all said and done, that year in the recovery house turned out to be the most valuable time I had ever spent. It is ironic because in my original writing I described my belief that when a person is totally at peace in his or her life using drugs is not necessarily a negative. When I wrote that I felt that I was at peace and maybe I was, but I certainly never foresaw the 5 years of suffering and drug abuse, followed by over a year of treatment all because I couldn't let go of the idea that I was still at peace all that time. I still believe that statement to be true although I do not know if it is possible or realistic. I know from my experience now that the natural high that comes from living honestly and with purpose far exceeds any high that I got from a drink or drug.

This is in no way a campaign to end drug or alcohol use around the world. I am confident that my years of getting high were crucial to my development and I would not trade them for anything. I had a lot of exciting and entertaining times over those years which I still look back on with fondness. My point is that after a time I realized that I had gotten all that I could from that method of release and wanted to experience something more rewarding and sustainable.

Living my life in alignment with who I was born to be and trying my best to adhere to the 10 principles I have written about can give me that sustainable pure high that I had always wanted. Obviously it is much easier said than done or else I would have avoided those years of turmoil and confusion. What matters is that whenever I or anyone decides to be who they are meant to be life becomes a joyous and authentic existence. Things happen without effort and stress, and life seems easy. The downside is that just as easily I or anyone can forget what works and mix up what is most important for them.

To a large extent I did lose track of what was most important after I completed the Miracle House program. In addition to drugs and alcohol, I can get overly wrapped up in relationships. Very soon after being set free from the strict rules which I had lived by for the previous year, I jumped into a serious relationship with someone I had seen and been attracted to the whole time that I had been in LA.

Just this fact alone was not a bad thing and what I went through as a whole was very valuable to me. It is just another example of how it is easy to lose track of who you are and what works best for you in day to day life. What happened very quickly was that my priorities shifted from working on myself and being an honest good person to spending as much time as I could with this person and keeping her happy.

This is very normal in new or really any relationship to remove focus from you and place it on the other person. The danger in doing this is that it allows you to live with things that under normal circumstances would be unacceptable to you. In this case I chose to put up with significant emotional pain stemming from jealousy issues that were present prior to our being together.

To make a long story short I fought my true nature and endured this pain because I put the well-being of this person ahead of my own. I made certain decisions and stayed in this relationship for 2 years because of fear and denial of my intuition. The fear came from my not wanting to hurt this person even though I was being hurt and was not happy with what was happening. On some level I knew that it was not working, but I stayed anyway which caused unnecessary levels of emotional pain to take place for both of us. If I had been true to myself from the start, both of us would have avoided the turbulent and very draining end to our relationship.

I certainly do not mean to imply that I regret being with this person. In fact she helped me grow immensely and the positive aspects of our time together were wonderful. The point is that because I put her feelings ahead of my own I lost sight of what was ultimately best for me. This is just another illustration of how people every day stray from their true nature. I do not consider the two years a mistake at all, but I am confident my life could have been easier if I had listened to my intuition rather than my fears.

The end of that relationship and all of the experiences that I had been through in the previous seven years gave me what I needed to update and rewrite the 10 chapters of this book. What follows are those 10 chapters in their new and improved form.

PART 2
UNCOVERING THE PATH

1

THE TRUTH IS
LIBERATING

The last section described the pain and suffering that my life consisted of as a result of my not being truthful to myself and others. I lost touch with the person that I once wanted to be, and took actions which made me feel as though I needed to lie. I was trapped by my inability to see my life for what it was and admit it to those around me. As I mentioned, it was not until I regained my perspective and started living an honest, life that I was liberated from that self-made prison.

This chapter is all about the importance of honesty or truth with both one's self and others.

This belief and practice is the foundation upon which all of the other lessons in this book are based. Until one is able to live authentically, the lessons will not have the power that they are intended to have. Living authentically means figuring out who you want to be and striving each day to become that person. It also means that you should have no reason to lie to others because your actions will not need to be hidden.

To begin I will give the most recent example from my life of not living authentically and what happened as a result. I was living on Martha's Vineyard and feeling as though I was not living up to my potential. My wife and I were trying to figure out a way to move off the island, as we felt as though we couldn't reach our career goals in such an isolated environment.

I decided to pursue a career in the financial services industry, specifically selling life insurance and investment products. After a few months of interviewing I landed a job with one of the well-known companies. I would be earning a salary to start off which would enable my family and I to move and pay the bills. I chose this line of work in part because of a lifelong fascination with investments and money. I also felt that I would be able to provide a valuable service to my future clients. I have to admit that the potential to make a lot of money and provide my family with a comfortable lifestyle was also a factor.

Things started off well for the most part. I was very enthusiastic and quickly began doing what I could to book appointments and talk to people. I went to networking events, called businesses, and spent hours on end dialing numbers to potential clients. In those first weeks I was easily able to convince myself that all of my efforts were for the purpose of helping.

As time passed I became more and more aware of the culture in which I was working. I found it difficult to truly be myself or speak about my actual beliefs. I noticed that I rarely heard people talking about how much they had helped someone that week, but very often about how much money they had made. At first I pushed these realizations aside and worked harder to see as many people as I could about their financial needs.

For a time I was successful at setting up and conducting appointments with potential customers. Even so, the longer I stayed with it the harder it was to ignore the fact that I was not being myself. I saw that in order to be deemed successful in this business it would be very difficult for me to be the person that I wanted to be. The feeling of uneasiness and conflict only strengthened over time and not surprisingly very few of my appointments turned into sales or clients.

It wasn't long before I dreaded going into the office, and I was terrified because I had moved my family in large part to pursue this new career. After a few months my initial salary was going to run out and I would be left with only the commissions from the handful of sales I had made. I was forced to make a decision; change careers again or force myself to try harder to go against my nature.

It wasn't easy considering I had a family to support and only a short time before I had been very excited about starting my new career. Nevertheless, I knew that I needed to make a change. Immediately after making that decision I felt a huge weight lifted from me, and I was confident that I had made the right choice. That being said, it was over 4 months before I could find another job. Those months were very difficult at times for me and my wife because we did not know how we were going to pay bills and tensions ran high most of the time.

Even so, I never lost faith that I had made the correct choice and it turned out that the time off enabled me to finish working on this book. In the end I wound up working at a male adolescent drug and alcohol treatment facility where I do what I can to help kids who are struggling in much the same way that I did at their age. I don't ever dread going into work, and I feel very fortunate that I listened to myself and moved on from a situation that did not allow me to live authentically.

This story is not an endorsement for every person who is not completely satisfied with their job to up and quit. Instead it is a clear example from my experience that shows if you make an honest effort to remain true to yourself the decisions you make will most likely end up working out favorably for you. As I said it was not an easy decision to make nor was it a quick and easy transition, but in the end I landed in a much better situation because my desire to be truthful to who I want to be was my focus.

Hopefully this example will give the reader a clear understanding of what I mean by the truth being liberating. The feeling of being unburdened when I made the decision to switch career paths is the liberation I wish to describe. Most individuals have a set of standards by which they try to live, and when those standards are not being met the individuals suffer in one form or another. It could be an overall feeling of uneasiness, constant mental stress, back pain, or stomach problems, the list could go on and on.

What most people don't realize is that most or all of those symptoms could be alleviated by living honestly in all areas of their lives. I focused on career and how not being true to myself led to strong emotional discomfort. This same principle could be applied to relationships, school, actions you take in your personal life, or anything else which causes a compromise in one's core values.

Take for example romantic relationships. Many can relate to a situation where they stay with a person that does not treat them well even though on some level they know the relationship is not healthy for them. The individual lies to themself by saying he/she treats me this way because they care, or I won't be able to find someone new so I might as well stay rather than risk being alone. By ignoring the truth, or that voice inside that says that they deserve better, they become trapped in an unsatisfying situation. The moment a person becomes honest with themself and makes the decision to leave they become liberated and have a chance to attract a compatible mate. (Keep in mind that until some inner changes are made the individual is likely to continue attracting the same type of partner.)

On the other end of the spectrum, there are those who stay in relationships where they are loved and respected but do not feel the same way about their partner. These individuals lead their significant other to believe that the feelings being shared are mutual when they are not. Over time this situation can be just as damaging because the relationship is based on a lie. The dishonest party may feel as though they are sparing the other person from pain, but the reality is that only the truth will liberate both parties. It is true that telling your partner the truth, in this case, will cause them pain especially if you have been together for a long time. Even so, the end result will be the opportunity for both parties to explore relationships wherein the feelings actually are mutual.

Any situation that causes one to feel as though they are not being true to themselves will be a hindrance to that person's wellbeing. It doesn't have to be as significant as a career choice or romantic relationship. Instances arise all the time where an individual is faced with a choice of whether or not to do what they feel is "right." Maybe you see someone being bullied and don't make an effort to help that person out. Maybe a cashier gives you too much change and you decide to take it rather than be honest. You may think that you won't be able to help the bullied person or that the store makes enough money already. Unfortunately over time those little instances build up and effect how you feel about yourself. Also you never know how significant one of those small choices is to the other person/people involved. Helping the bullied person could be seen as a huge gift to them and giving back the extra change could save that cashier's job because his/her drawer won't be short.

The examples like this could go on and on, but the point is that doing what feels right will most likely benefit you and anyone else who may be involved. Those gut feelings are the indicators which point to the true you. Thus far I have described instances where a person can and does become dishonest with themself. Very often when you are lying to yourself you end up lying to others as well.

I'm sure most of the readers know what it is like to tell a lie and then suffer the consequences. It starts off with a feeling of uneasiness. Next you may become uncomfortable around the person or people you lied to. Often the first lie will lead to others. In the end you are completely stressed and will have trouble keeping your story straight.

We go through all of that generally to avoid a very slight consequence or embarrassment in the moment. Wouldn't it be nice to never have to go through that ridiculous cycle? If you don't lie you won't have to. How often have you heard something to the effect of, "it wouldn't have been a problem if you had just told me in the first place?" Somehow we are able to convince ourselves that lying is the easy way out, when we know deep down that it only makes things harder. Save yourself untold amounts of stress and energy by being upfront with people about your actions and behaviors. (I am not suggesting that anyone tells someone that they look terrible or fat because they are asked and want to be honest. Although being honest may have the effect of hurting people at times, this is not a license to belittle people.)

In the end being honest with yourself and with others goes hand in hand. It is much more likely that you will find it easy to be honest with others if you are taking actions that coincide with who you want to be. Each day is an opportunity to live truthfully and grow. I encourage everyone to utilize those opportunities to determine who you want to be and strive towards being that person. You will never know what it feels like to be liberated by the truth until you decide to give it a try.

Exercise 1
Who am I?

This chapter and much of this book is about deciding who you want to be as a person and actually being that person. A good first step to making this goal a reality is to take the time and effort to articulate the person you want to be. This exercise allows you to do just that. Make a list of short sentences starting with the words "I am." Following the words I am write a word or words that you would use to describe your ideal character. For example:

I am intelligent
I am compassionate
I am Honest

Write as many sentences like this as you would like. Remember the words at the end should either describe traits that you currently exhibit and like about yourself or ones that you would like to exhibit. Place the list somewhere that you will remember to look at it every morning. You may also want to carry a copy of the list with you at all times so that you can look it over whenever you have a free moment. The purpose of this exercise is to bring to your consciousness all the traits that you feel would encompass your ideal character. As with anything the more you focus on these traits the more likely it will be that you start to exhibit them. Make this a consistent part of your routine and notice the changes that naturally occur.

Exercise 2
What I meant to say was……

This exercise is all about being honest no matter how trivial it may seem. Most of us can relate to exaggerating a story or completely making something up in order to join in a conversation. In this exercise you are asked to be your own informant. Very simply, as soon as you catch yourself saying something that isn't 100% true you will correct yourself. This act is meant to be somewhat embarrassing and humbling. Hopefully after fessing up a few times your desire to not have to do it anymore will keep you honest. You will most likely soon realize that you don't gain anything from warping the truth or making things up. The exercise is also meant to show the individual how often we bend the truth and don't realize it. You may think that small silly lies are inconsequential, but over time they can become the cause of negative feeling about one's self and lack of trust from others.

Exercise 3
An Honest Assessment

In this exercise you are going to further utilize your list from exercise 1. At least once a week, and preferably at the end of your day, take out your list and reflect on the week gone by. Look at each of the traits and try to remember an instance or more where you had the opportunity to exhibit the trait. Did you act the way you would want your ideal self to act, or did you fall short? Be honest, of course, and I suggest recording these assessments in some sort of journal so that you track the progress you have made over time. Give yourself ample time to really reflect and write down what comes to mind. Again like the other exercises this is about being aware of your actions and putting your focus upon being the person you desire to be. It is quite likely that when one starts this exercise there will many instances where the person feels that they have fallen short. This is ok as long as the individual stays committed to the exercise and makes progress over time. Also allow yourself to feel good about all the times where you did act as you hoped you would. It takes time, effort and focus to change behaviors so be patient and you will surely have more and more positive things to write in your weekly assessment.

2

LET KNOWLEDGE AND INTUITION GUIDE YOU (NOT FEAR)

With risk comes reward. Most of us have heard this simple cliché at some point in our lives. The question is how many of us have actually thought about the wisdom in this simple message? How many times have you avoided an idea or opportunity based on the amount of risk associated with it? How many times have you kicked yourself for not listening to your instincts, but rather the fear that came along with it?

This chapter is all about letting go of these irrational fears which hold countless people back from the lives which they desire. Living a fulfilling life free from regrets often means taking risks at times in spite of an apparent likelihood of failure. Ask yourself would you rather live a life that is "safe" but lacks passion, or would you like to wake up each day filled with excitement for the path you have chosen?

In observing the world in which we live, it has become apparent that so many of us base our life decisions around fear of the worst rather than the possibility of the best. We take jobs which we can barely tolerate in which our only solace is our two day weekend. Even some of that "free" time is wasted because our dread of going back does not allow us to enjoy what we are doing in the moment. All of this because we are afraid that we won't be able to find a career which uplifts us and brings us joy all the time. We become so entrenched in the idea that we won't have enough to pay the bills that we shut ourselves off from the endless possibilities which are always present if we are aware of them.

The same can be said for our romantic relationships. We stay in them well past the point of mutual happiness because of a fear of being alone. The false presumption that we won't find someone who enriches our lives makes us stay in relationships which are clearly not working. Wouldn't it be nice to come home to a person that you are excited to see and who feels the same about you? Why then do we settle for an existence where neither partner gets what they need? The answer again is fear. We convince ourselves that being unhappy but with somebody is better than the unknown of being alone and finding someone who is better for us.

It is my belief that every person deserves the life of their dreams. To me those dreams and aspirations which excite us are the indicators of the path we should follow in life. Most great achievements in life don't come by accident or without a great deal of patience and perseverance. If the thought of a goal brings with it a feeling of joy and excitement, then the pursuit of that goal is worthwhile. It seems to me that a majority of people sell themselves short on a daily basis. Their fears tell them to stay put, not rock the boat, and avoid change. All of this while the quieter voice of intuition is telling them that in order to have true happiness, risk, change, and growth are all necessary.

It is always possible that one's efforts will not bring about the outcome that one envisions. For me giving everything I have towards a goal and not succeeding is infinitely easier to live with than not trying at all. Often the goal will change along the way and you will see that what you had in mind was not the reality which you thought it was. This being said, you will never know unless you start taking those steps towards the life that you desire.

I have been talking exclusively about large life decisions, but you can apply this mindset to any situation. Every day we are faced with countless choices which come with some degree of risk. Talking to that guy or girl you have a crush on but who you think is "too good for you," speaking up in a meeting with an idea which could be ridiculed, raising your hand in class with a question that some might think is stupid. We decide not to do all of these things each day because of the chance of feeling some level of pain or embarrassment. Instead we might assume that the person wants to talk to us, the idea you have will gain you the respect of your coworkers, and the question will not only help you but also others who had the same question but were also too afraid to ask.

If you really stop to think about it, there are countless instances where fear prevents us from doing things which could benefit ourselves and others. We must find a way to make our decisions from the place of inspiration rather than fear. It takes practice and may even feel as though you are going against your instincts for a time, but eventually you will see that an initial impulse is most likely the right one and the fear that follows is unwarranted.

Now I will share an example from my life which illustrates the points I am trying to make. It is the pursuit of the publication of this book. This journey started when I was 17 years old and about half way through my junior year of High school. The initial decision to write this book came with the decision to leave High School.

I did just that and obviously there were significant fears from both within myself and the people I was closest to at the time. The feeling that it was the absolute right thing to do for me at that time won out over the fear of failure and being left without even a High School diploma. I did end up finishing High School after what I refer to as the completion of the first draft of this book. Nonetheless it could not be a reality today if I had not listened to my initial intuition.

I described in detail in the previous section of the book what happened during the years following the completion of that first draft. I give this example because even though one's first efforts at accomplishing a life goal did not work out does not mean one should abandon the goal. It has been many years since I was a junior in High school and I have endured a lot of disappointment and disheartening experiences along the way. I see now that all of those seemingly insignificant and disappointing experiences are what became the fuel and material for the final draft of this volume.

Pursuing a dream does not necessarily mean quitting everything that you are doing now to find instant success. Most of us will need to both support our basic needs while simultaneously moving towards our desired reality. Ask the most successful and happy people on Earth if they just fell backwards into their achievements. For most it was a steady climb with varying degrees of success along the way. Remember that all things worthwhile in life come with determination and perseverance. In fact the common element connecting all successful people is their ability to disregard failure and fear to keep moving forward. The only person who can ever truly hold you back from your goals is you.

I am not saying that all endeavors such as this will end happily. What I can say is once you have learned to be true to yourself, most often those gut feelings will lead you in the right direction. Conversely, listening to fears will most often lead to disappointment and a feeling of missing out on life's many gifts. As I said, we determine the course of our own journey, and the choice is ours as to whether one wants everything the world has to offer or something less.

I will now give 3 exercises that should help the reader to see the reality of our imagined fears and just how much they affect us each day.

Exercise 1
"I Shoulda Done That"

For the next week keep a record of every time you want to do something but don't because of some form of fear. Be as honest and accurate as you can and try to record the situation and what exactly held you back. By the end of the week you should see patterns and have a better understanding of how often fear controls your life.

Exercise 2
"Yes Man or Woman"

For one day you must say yes to every request that is asked of you. From Karaoke, to dancing, to helping someone move for one day the answer must be yes. Of course if the request is illegal or carries with it a high risk of bodily harm it is advisable to decline. This exercise should show you that no matter what you are asked to do you will survive and more than likely enjoy yourself more than you anticipated. It takes the decision out of your hands so that fear cannot decide for you.

Exercise 3
"For all the Single Ladies and Gentlemen"

Most of you single people out there have at least that one person you see regularly and want to get to know but are too afraid to do so. Well in this exercise you are asked to simply approach them and start a friendly conversation. The worst that will happen is that the conversation will go nowhere and that will be the end of it. But it is also possible that you will start a meaningful relationship with the man or woman of your dreams. Either way the practice is about letting go of irrational fears that hold you back. Again it is worse to live not knowing what could have been than to be turned down and move on. Have fun with it and soon you should be able to talk to anyone without apprehension.

3

FIND BEAUTY ALL
AROUND YOU

We live a world that is filled with miraculous creations. Why is it that so much of our focus is placed on the negative aspects in our lives? It's cold out, the economy stinks, this traffic is so frustrating. These are the thoughts and things that we tend to put emphasis on each day.

Imagine if most of our focus was placed on the beauty that surrounds us all. This simple shift in perspective would unleash a vast supply of positive energy which is always present yet goes untapped. If we believe that the world is what we make of it, then let's make it the wondrous awe inspiring place that it is. This chapter is all about finding the things which you see as beautiful and giving a larger portion of your time and attention to them.

When discussing beauty I will break it into four distinct categories. They include physical beauty that you find in another person, intellectual beauty which you find in a belief or idea, creative beauty found in manmade creations, and natural beauty which are the wonders of nature. All four aspects have their value and when you start to see the world more for its positive attributes than its negative, increased energy and happiness are sure to follow.

First let's discuss the beauty we find in another person's appearance. I do not want to imply that a relationship can or should be built solely around physical attraction. Nevertheless we should face the reality that it is uplifting to be with someone whom we are physically attracted to. Physical chemistry is a part of all successful and happy romantic relationships.

The point here is to see our surroundings as miraculous creations, and that includes the people in our lives. It is hard to dismiss the idea that it feels good to be around people whom we see as beautiful. For those of us who are in relationships with others we are not physically attracted to it may be a good idea to look at the reasons why. Sometimes a lack of communication or a history of arguing can lead to seeing our partner as less appealing than when we met. Whatever the reason, this lack of chemistry is an indication that something must change. Either the problems must be dealt with in order to restore the flame or else separation may be the best solution for both parties. Remember that feelings are our most valuable indicators to the truth, so not feeling attracted to the person you are with should not be ignored.

Relationships should always be a source of positive energy and comfort. If you do not see your partner as attractive it is unlikely you will be able to get past that to access that positive energy. It may seem trivial and shallow but there is nothing wrong with seeking out a partner that you are physically drawn to. Again staying with someone merely for the sake of not being alone will not benefit either party. Ideally coming home to your significant other after a hard day should lift your spirits just by looking at them. If this is not the case then some examination may be necessary to figure out if you are with the right person. Many times a shift in perspective is all that is needed. Every person is beautiful in his or her own way, so we must try to see that rather than focus on a negative quality which gets our attention.

After getting past physical appearance the arguably more important factor is what I call intellectual beauty. We all know that it is enjoyable to find common ground with people who share our beliefs. It is just as beneficial to be around people you believe have beautiful thoughts and ideas as it is to be around people you think have beautiful appearances.

I too often observe people who go against their core beliefs in order to find acceptance. It is most often recognized as peer pressure in school environments, but it is a problem that affects individuals of all ages in all settings. I believe that these individuals have the false perception that by agreeing with actions or ideas regardless of their own true belief they will find the comfort and lift that comes from being accepted. The actual result is that these people are drained rather than lifted because they are fighting against their true nature.

Once we figure out who we are and are true to ourselves, it will become evident that this false acceptance is not what we want. The energy we can gain from truly being around like-minded people is immensely uplifting. There is no need to pretend when it comes to your belief system because once you are comfortable with who you are you will attract the same.

I strongly encourage everyone to spend time with people you admire. There is strength in numbers and it is a great aid to have friends and partners who you can share ideas and dreams with. Beauty does not have to come in tangible form. As you have probably experienced, hearing a great idea or having your own validated is a very powerful experience.

This chapter is all about seeking and finding beauty everywhere. It is quite possible that the people who will end up inspiring and uplifting you the most are right in front of you now. If you do not feel excited and optimistic conversing with or being around your friends then maybe they are not the best friends for you.

I cannot say that all the people I call friends share all of my beliefs. What I can say is that I always feel better after interacting with them. It is this unseen beauty which we should seek out. Again once you start making the effort to be true to yourself great people will start to enter your life. If we all need support at times in our lives why not receive it from individuals you admire?

The beauty we find in manmade creations is yet another area we can gain positivity. Think about all the time we spend dwelling on the dirty bathroom, dented car door, or trash lined street on which we live. It is obvious that being subjected to a dirty or cluttered environment can take away from one's peace of mind. Why not use the opposite logic to our benefit. When we clean up or beautify the places we most often inhabit it is much easier to relax and find inspiration at any given time.

I for one know organization and tidiness are not my strong suits. I often let clutter and unneeded objects pile up in my car and living space. I have also noticed that when I am constantly subjected to these areas which are not in order, (lack of beauty) I find it much more difficult to relax and concentrate. Just by taking the time to clean up and organize the places I spend most of my time, I feel as though I can breathe easier and get the beneficial energy and inspiration I need to be productive from day to day.

I can say confidently that keeping your house, car, or office in order will lead to having your thoughts, emotions and actions in order as well. Many times we overlook the simple act of tidying up not realizing that by living in this sort of chaos we are not fully allowing ourselves to rest and recharge. I have often told myself that I am too tired to clean up, and that I will get to it later. Ironically the mess itself may be the explanation for my lack of energy. By just doing the chore right away, I alleviate both the mess and the lethargy.

As a complement to keeping your home or office neat, bringing artwork or furnishings that you find beautiful will also add to your level of serenity when in those spaces. Most of us have an opinion on what looks good, whether it be a couch, rug or painting. If so, make an effort to bring those elements into your living areas. Surrounding yourself in manmade beauty can only raise your level of enjoyment and peace when at home.

I know firsthand that this goal costs money and many times we must make do with what is available to us financially. I also know that there are inexpensive ways to bring beauty into our homes while achieving the same results as purchasing big ticket items. Yard sales, flea markets, and estate sales are all great places to find valuable items at very low prices. Framing and enlarging your own photos can also replace purchasing expensive artwork and has the added benefit of sentimental value. Of course it never hurts to check clearance racks and "going out of business sales" as well. The object here is to bring in as many beautiful elements as you can to your home so that being there provides you with a place of enjoyment and peace. Don't underestimate the value of being aesthetically pleased.

I cannot forget music and literature as they are manmade creations as well. It is undeniable that listening to great music or reading a great book has the power to completely change your state of mind for the better. I encourage everyone to spend some time listening to your favorite music every day. Also find creative beauty in literature   and you will add to your serenity and overall wellbeing.

Last we come to nature, our most abundant source of beauty. I cannot stress enough how beneficial it can be to body, mind and spirit to go outside and appreciate the natural wonders of the world. It is mind boggling the intricacy and perfection that makes up our natural world. If you allow it, nature can energize and inspire any time you wish.

It amazes me how often in our busy lives we become oblivious to the beauty of our planet. We get caught up in deadlines, bills, homework, appointments, etc. Often we get overwhelmed by everything we must get done because we are neglecting our inner nature.

I can admit that I have lived in some of the most beautiful places in the world and didn't even think twice about it. I was so caught up in my life and its self-made problems that I ignored the treasures which surrounded me. Spending 15 minutes in nature and reflecting on its beauty is often all someone needs to shift their perspective and get through difficult situations. It is only when we ignore all the beautiful creations of our world that we become stressed out by our day to day humdrum lives.

As I said, when our focus is primarily on the things that we find objectionable they become the things that we attract into our reality. Shifting our attention to what is beautiful in our lives empowers us to introduce more beauty to us and gives us the energy we need to overcome any challenge with which we are faced.

Everyone is drawn to different aspects of nature. For some it is water, flowers, stars or trees. There is no wrong way to appreciate the natural wonders of the world. Whatever uplifts you the most should become a significant focus of your attention and part of your routine. Go for a hike, sit by the ocean, or gaze at the stars and allow the beauty that you see to melt away the tension which is generally present in both your conscious and subconscious mind.

Nothing I describe could be easier than spending at least a little bit of time in nature on a regular basis. At first you may feel like you have no time as it is. Soon you will see that when attention is placed elsewhere those activities which used to occupy all your time and energy can be accomplished quicker and more efficiently. When we are drained by the responsibilities in our lives it seems as if we never have a moment to breathe. Take several moments to breathe in the beauty of our planet and you will feel ready for whatever else may be going on for you.

Before I give the exercises for this chapter I must touch on one vital point. I have focused exclusively on the beauty we find outside of ourselves in this chapter. To optimize the benefits we will receive from these sources of beauty we must first see ourselves as beautiful. By being true to who you are and not letting fear determine your life's path you will be well on your way to seeing yourself as the miracle that you are. Once you see yourself in this way the world around you will become that much brighter and more beautiful in your eyes.

Exercise 1
"Create Beauty"

This exercise is fun and simple for anyone even if you do not think that you have a creative bone in your body. All you do is choose a creative activity and put your whole effort and attention on completing it. There are those who are artistically inclined, so maybe they could paint a picture or do a charcoal sketch. Some like to build things, so they may build a table or bookcase. For musicians it could mean writing an original piece of music, and for writers it could mean a poem, short story, or even free hand journal writing. The point here is to take your focus away from the things which most often occupy your time and focus and put that attention on creating something beautiful. Depending on the complexity of the project you choose you may not be able to finish it in one sitting. Even so, make a commitment to putting all your effort into working on your project when you are actually working on it. I'm sure anyone who tries this exercise will enjoy both the process and the end result. Remember to have fun and be present and you will surely create something with lasting beauty.

Exercise 2
"Spring Cleaning"

This exercise is exactly what you think it is. Spend an afternoon or night cleaning up your living space. Get rid of all the things you don't use or need anymore, donating what you can. It's amazing how much more peace and rejuvenation you will find in your home once it is free from clutter and mess.

After you have taken on this major project make an effort to keep this standard of living.

Exercise 3
"Be One With Nature"

Take at least 20 minutes and find a place outdoors which you find beautiful. Keep your eyes open and try to fully relax. Notice the sounds, sights, smells, and feeling of being present in those moments. Try not to think about obligations during this time and allow the beauty of your surroundings to heal your body mind and soul. Reflect on the unbelievable creative power of the Universe, which you are now looking at. Notice how your mood and emotions have changed once your time is up.

These exercises will be more beneficial the more you practice them. In time you will see the world around you as an infinite source of beauty and energy at your disposal.

4

TAKE TIME FOR
YOURSELF

Many of us spend so much time worrying about our responsibilities and the welfare of others that we neglect our own. I know personally that I have often been more concerned with how others would be affected by my actions than how I would be affected. By no means do I think it is wrong to be mindful of the feelings and interests of others, but if by doing so you become drained, no one benefits. This chapter is all about learning to take the time you need for yourself so that when it comes time to be there for others you are capable.

It seems to me that this fast paced instantly gratifying world we live in, (at least in this country), devalues doing nothing at times. We are taught not to waste time and consequently often feel as though we do not have enough time each day to take a break. This mentality of constant motion and productivity leads to stress, burn out, irritability and general lack of appreciation for the simple things in life. What's the point of doing and achieving so much if you do not even have a moment to enjoy it?

In addition to not wanting to "waste time" we feel like it is selfish to tell our loved ones or peers that we need some time alone. This is especially true of parents raising young children. I can understand why someone would feel that time spent alone was a selfish act but I don't view it that way. I believe that everyone needs time to recharge in order to give their family, friends, coworkers or classmates their best.

Sometimes sitting quietly and doing nothing can be the most productive and self-less action you can take. Often it is when we are constantly looking to do things or cater to others that we get overwhelmed and stuck. By overworking we can compound the problem by forcing the issue, stressing about falling behind or any number of false realities we create for ourselves. The truth is that if we step back, take some time to reflect and recharge, it is likely that we can achieve the same results with much less effort. If you are constantly in full throttle it is impossible to see that all you may need to get over the hump is 30 minutes away from it all.

I also know from experience that when I constantly give of myself and not to myself, I become drained and resentful. Rather than being uplifted by helping another, I get no enjoyment because I have stretched myself too thin. Again declining just one request in exchange for some quality "me" time will restore that energy and perspective so that I can give freely and fully again. I am in no way endorsing a life of solitude, merely a practical incorporation of a little bit of alone time into your current routine.

In my experience no less than 15 minutes and no more than an hour are needed to achieve a significant level of relaxation and rejuvenation. Again no one is asking you to neglect any of your current responsibilities, it is about setting aside some enjoyable time for yourself so that those responsibilities are easier to handle. For many of you it may have been quite a while since you actually set aside half an hour for yourself. If this is true you probably don't realize how beneficial that time alone can be.

No matter how busy you think you are I believe everyone can find at least 15 minutes and hopefully a little more. For those of you with small children or other nonstop responsibilities, ideally you will have someone there to take the burden for this short time each day. It may also feel awkward and difficult to get away from it all at first, but in time I know it can be incorporated into any routine. The more you nurture yourself the less likely you are to get overwhelmed by the everyday stressors you encounter.

After you have established that you can set aside some alone time for yourself, the next step is to choose what you want to do with the time. There is no wrong answer to this question. My only suggestion is to do something that will allow you to relax and get your mind away from your normal thought patterns. Your goal is to rejuvenate yourself so that after the time is up you are refreshed and ready to handle all comers.

Some simple suggestions are take a walk, read, meditate, listen to music, or take a bath. Instincts should tell you what the best use of this time is each day, so do whatever feels right. Again the only requirement is to be by yourself and to let go of the usual things which occupy your thoughts. Hopefully you will recognize the immediate benefit of this short break from the world and you will look forward to it each day.

Another suggestion I have is to shut off your cell phone and not check email during this time. This is a personal practice, so if possible really detach yourself from any potential distractions. I understand some people may be on call or need a phone because a loved one is sick, but be honest with yourself because 10-15 years ago none of us had cell phones and we all survived. Ideally it will feel liberating to unplug for a short time.

It is also important to inform the people who may be looking for you that you will not be available during your chosen time. Explain the purpose of your absence and I'm sure they will understand. In addition it is likely they will notice a positive change in your demeanor once taking time for yourself is an established part of your life. Ultimately we want everyone in your life to feel good about your decision to nourish yourself. In fact you can be an example to others around you who are overwhelmed and never seem to take a break.

As I've said, feelings of guilt or that you are wasting valuable time are likely to arise at first. Push past these feelings and the way you feel and interact with others will prove that you are doing the right thing. It's all about working smarter not harder, and this down time allows for a more productive, efficient, and happy you.

Here are the 3 exercise for this chapter. They should help get the ball rolling on your new commitment to yourself.

Exercise 1
"Put it in your Calendar"

If you are having trouble finding time to be by yourself, simply make time. Schedule it into your day, literally. Consider it a meeting with yourself and do not miss your meeting. It may sound silly but if you do not make this practice a priority it is unlikely to work for you. Whatever you need to do, whether it be writing it in a calendar, setting an alarm, or simply making it the same time each day commit to rejuvenating your mind body and spirit. Let your friends and families know that you have this appointment and stick to it. If you do soon you will not need a reminder because you will cherish this time.

Exercise 2
"Just Breathe"

This exercise is for those new to meditation who would like to incorporate that as part of their routine. It is a basic mindfulness meditation technique which is easy to follow. In short, find a comfortable seated position in a way which allows for relaxed full breaths. After you are comfortable start to breathe, preferably through the nose. Your object is to keep your breath as your only focus of attention. When you inhale be aware that you are inhaling, perhaps noticing the feeling of air entering your nostrils. Do the same as you are exhaling. Do not be concerned if thoughts arise and you lose track of your breath. This is almost inevitably going to happen no matter how long you practice. When a thought comes and you become aware that you have lost attention to your breath, acknowledge this fact and return your focus to your inhaling and exhaling. In the beginning time will seem to move very slowly so try a length of time which feels comfortable to you. If this is your first experience with meditation, five minutes may be enough. The hope is that with practice your stream of thoughts will slow down and separate, allowing you to spend more time in the present moment and less time thinking about countless other distractions. I make an effort to meditate each day and feel that it allows me to relax and appreciate all of my other activities more deeply.

Exercise 3
"Just say No"

Not to be confused with an anti-drug campaign or our previous yes man exercise. This is for the people who feel obligated to take on any request regardless of how it affects their own wellbeing. Very simply practice saying no to people when you truly need to. Helping someone else at your own expense isn't really helpful if you think about it. This chapter is about nourishing you in order to nourish others. It's a great practice to be of service to people, but not when you become depleted as a result. Learn to say no at times and keep your own wellbeing in mind and most likely you will not have to decline very many requests at all.

5

ACCEPT OTHERS BELIEFS WHILE KEEPING YOUR OWN

So much of the turbulence in today's world revolves around our inability to put ourselves in someone else's shoes. We become so entrenched in our beliefs and way of doing things that we lose sight of the fact that there are other options. If we are Democrats, then Republicans are wrong, if we are Catholic, Jewish people are wrong, and so on down the line. The truth is that both sides can be right at the same time. It is alright to have a different view or opinion. It is when that view is perceived as a threat that wars, hate, violence and intolerance prevail.

I believe that it is fine to have strong opinions, but with that comes the realization that other people can have strong opinions even if they aren't the same as mine. I would never want someone to change what they believe on account of what I believe and vice versa. Adopting someone else's point of view is much different than accepting someone else's point of view. In reality your life is not changed by someone else seeing the world in a different way unless you let it.

In most cases an individual's belief system comes about as a result of their upbringing and the environment from which they came. Keeping this in mind is critical to accepting the huge spectrum of world views that exist. What is normal and practiced in one country or even neighborhood can and often does vary greatly from that of another. When we can acknowledge these differences in life circumstances and environments it makes it a little easier to see why opinions and beliefs are not universal. It makes little sense to hate or resent someone for believing what their life and the people around them have taught them to believe.

Take for example two individuals who grew up in different neighborhoods of Bridgeport, CT. The first person grew up in an area where poverty and crime were the norm. The other person was raised only a few minutes away but in an area where large homes, minimal crime, and economic abundance were considered normal. Geographically the two are almost identical. Beyond that these two people most likely see the world in very different ways.

The first person may grow up believing that life is always a struggle for survival. He will probably have a true appreciation for the basic necessities. He may also resent others who don't have to worry about money or crime. On the other hand the person around the corner may see life as easy and sheltered. She will likely take the basics in life for granted. She may resent people who don't have what she has because she thinks it is easy and normal to obtain monetary wealth.

These individuals are geographically linked, but you can see that they will have very different experiences at least early on in life. Neither one of them is wrong to see the world the way they do because that is what experience and the influential people in their lives have shown them. We are all products of our parents, relatives, peers, circumstances, and surroundings. This again should help make it easier to accept other's beliefs.

Clearly if two people from the same city can have completely different outlooks on life, then when you widen the gap extreme differences can arise. Think how different you would be if your life started in a third world country ruled by a dictator instead of your home town. Most likely your views on the world and even the United States would be completely different. My point again is that what we hear, see and experience shapes what we become as we age.

We are trying to arrive at an acceptance of any belief based on the fact that it came from a lifetime of events rather than from birth. I of course do not agree with hate, discrimination, inequality, or violence of any kind. I strongly oppose racism, war and tyrannical rule. What I can't say for sure is that if I was raised by different parents in a different place that I would still have all of the same beliefs. As opposed to agreeing with any of those behaviors I can accept that the people involved were taught that what they believed was true as well.

It does not do me or anyone else any good to have negativity about what anyone else thinks or does. Negativity can only compound itself, it cannot solve a problem. The truth is that hating someone for being a racist is no better than hating someone because they have a different color skin. Hate is hate no matter what reason is behind it. It is not realistic for everyone to agree but I believe that it is possible for everyone to agree to disagree.

Just think of all the extreme measures that have been taken as a result of differences in opinion. Wars over religious differences, racial differences, and political differences have been around since any of those things have existed. It can range from bullying in elementary school to attempts at genocide, and it all boils down to a lack of understanding and acceptance in one way or another. In short, accepting the wide array of upbringings, belief systems, and ideologies as they are is a huge step towards diminishing the physical and emotional abuse which dominates the news each day.

I am in no way saying that accepting things like hate crimes, oppression of women or children, or fanatical terrorist acts is easy. Acceptance is a practice and not something that usually comes all at once. It may be easier to accept small things like differing favorite music genres or sports teams. Remember that the practice is not to agree with everyone else but to realize that there are different ways to look at things generally based upon the environment and conditions in which you were raised. It is quite possible that you will never accept violent crime as understandable. Even so be aware that not accepting or hating someone for an action they have taken is not a solution. That negativity towards the problem can and will only create more of the same.

In practicing acceptance of other's beliefs it is likely that your beliefs will begin to change. Everything is always changing so why not allow your belief system to do the same. Having a fluid belief system lessens the chances of building up resentments based on an opposing point of view. It has been my observation that most of the hate and negativity in the world comes from those who have an extreme and rigid world view. For me it is best to stay somewhere in the middle so that I can grow and change as time passes.

I have been speaking exclusively about acceptance of others beliefs thus far. The seemingly much less challenging aspect of this chapter is about keeping your own. Most of us like to think we are strong in our convictions and do not let the opinions of others sway us. This may be true but I know that many times in my life I have let outside influences effect how I acted. I have definitely agreed with things merely for the sake of not rocking the boat. This is not at all uncommon but does contradict with my belief that you should always be true to yourself.

I did mention that having a fluid belief system is generally the best practice. Here I am more talking about core values which for the most part will stay with you throughout your life. Agreeing with things that go against those core values is where trouble can and does arise. Once you have a good working understanding of the first two chapters of this book you will be less susceptible to these compromises in values.

That being said, it is a practice just like acceptance. Most people do not like to appear different or go against the grain in a group setting. A common example is when a topic of conversation comes up in a group and you have an opposing view to everyone else involved. I know that I have gone along with the crowd in that situation and it may seem like the best or easiest thing to do in the moment. Unfortunately in the end I felt that I let myself down for not expressing how I really felt about the topic.

It is always best to be who you are and say what you believe. Often times you will not really be the only person with that view because others are afraid to speak out as well. Be proud of who you are and what you believe and you will see that your fear of speaking out or disagreeing is not warranted.

Hopefully we can agree that a world in which people can peacefully coexist despite their many differences is a goal worth striving towards. The basis of this book is about finding who you are, and trying to be that person each day. This chapter focuses more on allowing everyone else the same chance. We all have a right to believe what we want to believe, so make sure you let everyone in your life fulfill that right while remaining true to who you want to be. Here are some exercises to aid you in this process.

Exercise 1
"Knowledge is Power"

It seems as though most conflicts arise out of a lack of understanding of the opposing point of view. In this exercise you will make an effort to understand the people or beliefs which cause you resentment. If you hate people from Afghanistan because of the 9/11 tragedies learn about the culture and people of that nation. When people with different religious views bother you learn about those religions which you don't understand to diminish those negative feelings. In most cases you will find that the negativity you have towards a particular group is not justified. The more you know about differing cultures and world views the less likely you are to harbor resentments against them. Again this is not an exercise in changing what you believe, but rather learning to accept those things which you don't understand.

Exercise 2
"One Love"

Ultimately my goal for humanity is to have love and compassion for everyone. In this reality hostility over differences would melt away. This exercise is about cultivating that love and compassion within you and broadening that feeling to all mankind. It is a meditation technique specifically for the purpose of increasing compassion and seeing everyone as an equal. Start off as you would with any meditation focusing on the breath and allowing your mind to settle. After you are relaxed and focused, bring someone to mind who you love. Try as best you can to really experience and feel the love you have for that person. It could be a spouse, child, parent, friend or anyone that brings this feeling of love to the surface for you. Once you have that feeling strong in your heart direct that love towards yourself. Feel what it is like to be loved. After a couple of minutes like this, think of someone in your life who is suffering in some way. On your inhalation imagine taking their suffering and dissolving it in your now open heart. Some may want to visualize your heart space glowing with white or blue light and the suffering as being a dark cloud. On your exhalation imagine sending that person what it is they need to combat their suffering. Whether it is awareness, confidence, love, understanding or compassion, spend a few minutes breathing in this person's suffering and replacing it with what they need on the exhalation. Next do the same process but extend it to a larger group such as your neighborhood or hometown. Take in their suffering, let it dissolve in your heart, and replace it with love and compassion. You could say I take my town's suffering on the inhalation and I send them love and compassion on the exhalation. After doing this for a few minutes extend the practice out to all of mankind. It is important to consciously include the people whom you consider enemies or just people you do not like. Take in the worlds suffering and replace it with love and compassion. Again some may like to visualize this process. In time this practice should help to decrease your resentments and increase your ability to see the connection that exists between all people.

Exercise 3
"Get up Speak Up"

This exercise takes the example I gave earlier and puts it into practice. The next time you are in a group situation speak your truth whether or not it goes with the popular opinion. It is very important to always be true to who you are and what you believe in your core. The more you practice this the easier it will become and the better you will feel about yourself.

6

ENCOURAGE OTHER'S DREAMS

Have you ever had someone in your life that truly believed in you and encouraged you to pursue your goals? If so would you consider this person an important and powerful influence on your life path? Wouldn't you like to be able to be that person for others? This chapter is all about the importance of recognizing others dreams and doing what you can to help make those dreams a reality.

To me dreams and goals are precious indicators as to the course one's life should take. Without them, existence can become simply a routine in which our only goal is to pay the bills. We lose excitement and anticipation which is not healthy for our spirit. Although it is important to appreciate everything you have in the present moment, setting your sights on life goals helps to keep you moving forward and growing as an individual.

It is my belief that the more you give to the world the more you will receive. Giving someone the motivation and or assistance towards achieving what he/she wants is as big a gift as can be given. Imagine a world in which a majority of people were living out their dreams. This world would no doubt be less riddled with negativity and conflict than it is today. I realize that most people will not be able to affect the lives of a majority of individuals on Earth. Help where you can and hopefully those you help will do the same. Similarly to the theory in the movie, "Pay it Forward", the ripple effect you cause can be quite significant. Simply, the more people who have a focus on encouraging other's dreams the better off everyone will be.

In addition to the great feeling that comes from being generous and supportive it is much more likely that you will attract people into your life that will be willing to do the same for you. As I said the more you give the more you will receive. The point is not to help others in order to help yourself but you will see that this occurs naturally. Most of the great successes had at least one person along the way who pushed them or guided them to their goal. If you are fortunate enough to be that inspiration for someone else, then that will be reward enough.

As I've said, the more people in the world who are living their dreams the better off everyone is. Why not actively contribute to making that fact a reality. Each interaction you have with another person is an opportunity to make either a positive or negative impression. Doesn't it make sense to strive to have all of your interactions be positive for you and the other people involved? Giving someone a helping hand or the encouragement they need towards reaching their life's goals is an enormous act of generosity.

Have you ever been around someone who was very enthusiastic about the work they do and the life they live? Did it make you envious, jealous, or annoyed to see someone so happy? If so I can assure you that that person had help along the way, and that you have the same ability to be that happy too. Staying stuck in the mindset that you don't have what you want, and therefore shouldn't help other people, will only bring you more discontent. By your taking action to put another person's dreams ahead of your own even for a short while will change your perspective and likely your ability to accomplish your own life goals.

In my experience a majority of the most successful and happiest people are more than willing to share advice, encouragement, and time with those seeking a similar path. The reason for this is that these people know that they had mentors along the way as well. Also the happiest people realize that the more happiness there is in the world the better. If the individuals you aspire to be like see the value in assisting others towards their dreams then surely you should too. We are all in this world together so make the effort to improve the quality of life for everyone.

Here are some exercises to help incorporate encouragement of others into your routine.

Exercise 1
"Be a Big Brother or Sister"

This can mean literally volunteering at the agency with that name or simply taking a young person under your wing. Young people are generally full of ideas and dreams while also being very impressionable. Spending time with youth can be hugely beneficial to both you and them. It is unfortunate that not all children can obtain the guidance and encouragement they deserve from their own family. If you can provide that for a child you will be giving them a gift that they most likely will never forget. Again this person can be referred to you through a social service agency or be someone you know who may be in need of a role model. To help even one child believe in him/herself enough to pursue their dreams is a priceless service to the world.

Exercise 2
"Donate Wisely"

This exercise is for those of you who feel you do not have adequate time to give to an individual. In this exercise you simply make a charitable contribution to either the scholarship fund of a particular school or to an organization which provides assistance to students attempting to go to any school. A college degree is a big step towards the dreams of millions of school age students. Many of those students would not have the opportunity to get that degree without the aid of some sort of scholarship. By donating in this way you are anonymously helping the future of a deserving young person.

Exercise 3
"Valuable Experience"

For every person out there with an established career of one's choice there are thousands of young people who hope to do what you do. This exercise is about sharing your experience in order to help some of them to that end. Whether you are a sales professional, doctor, lawyer, or teacher the experience you have gained over the years is valuable to someone looking to walk a similar path. In this exercise you will actively attempt to find people most likely in high school or college who might benefit from your experience. Most high schools would be happy to have volunteer speakers come and talk to students about possible career paths. Preferably you will speak to students who specifically want to hear what you have to say. If you have a college nearby, volunteer to talk to students who are majoring in a field which relates to what you do. Whether the information you provide reinforces a person's desire to follow in your footsteps, or makes them change their mind, you are providing a valuable service. You may offer interested parties the opportunity to watch you in action so they can get an accurate picture of what they are striving for. Whatever you can do to help someone formulate and achieve their goals is a great and noble initiative.

7

SICKNESS IS A MENTAL AND EMOTIONAL MANIFESTATION

Have you ever found yourself so stressed out over work, money, a relationship or anything else that your physical health started to suffer? Most of us have but we rarely acknowledge that one event relates to the other. The truth is you cannot think, do, or experience anything without simultaneously affecting your mind, body, and spirit. Realizing this fact is a large step towards minimizing the amount of physical ailments you experience throughout your life.

Do you ever wonder why some people you know never seem to get sick? They are exposed to all of the same germs as you and others around you but are not affected in the same way. You may think that they simply have a stronger immune system than most. This is true but the reason they have a stronger immune system is not based strictly on their physical make-up. Almost without exception these people believe that they are not going to get sick. In addition they are generally happy, optimistic, and manage stress well.

Contrast this with the person who always seems to be fighting a cough, sniffle, or headache. Generally you will find the exact opposite of the person who is almost always healthy. They believe they are going to get sick if anyone around them does. They worry about sickness, are generally more pessimistic, and do not manage stress in a healthy way. Examined in this way it is easy to see why one person could differ from another so greatly in respect to staving off mild illness.

Most of us fall somewhere in between these two extremes. If given the choice I believe everyone would rather be more like the person who always seems healthy. Fortunately when you decide to believe that your physical health is largely determined by your mental attitude you are given this choice. Anyone is capable of being more positive, believing they can stay healthy, and minimizing their stress levels.

The problem is that most of us do not realize the power we have to affect our own health. We don't see that by focusing on someone else with a cold we attract the same to us, or that trying to do too much too fast will deplete our body's ability to maintain balance. It takes real effort to change our thought patterns and listen to our bodies when they need rest. If you constantly tell yourself that you are happy and healthy most likely you will be. If you see yourself as vulnerable to illness the likelihood is that you will get sick. Also if you are overexerting yourself, (aka stressing yourself out) the body will tell you in subtle ways before full blown illness appears.

You may experience a dull headache, an overall feeling of sluggishness, or a back ache. All of these are indicators that something is out of balance within your mind body spirit relationship. If you can address the issue before it goes any further you can spare yourself of more extreme discomfort and longer recovery time. Most often all you need in these early stages is proper nutrition and some fully rejuvenating rest.

Unfortunately most people resign to falling ill from time to time and do not heed the early warning signs of over stress which their bodies provide. This combination undoubtedly results in many illnesses which could have been avoided completely. I don't want to imply that if you think positively and have low stress levels that you are invulnerable to illness.

The point is that we all have a high degree of control as to how vulnerable we are based on these two factors.

If it sounds too simplistic to be true just evaluate your own experience. Can you remember getting sick during a time of unusual stress and turmoil? Have you ever obsessively worried about getting the flu or some other ailment and then gotten it? If you take an honest look I am confident that you will see a direct correlation between your physical wellbeing, and your thinking and stress management.

Even if you are not consciously thinking about getting sick, any negative thoughts and emotions decrease your body's ability to stay healthy. Take for instance if you are constantly dreading going to work or school. It becomes far more likely that you will be vulnerable to a cold or virus because you are basically telling yourself that you don't want to do the things that you have to do. If given this message your body's only option for granting your wish is to create illness. I am sure most of you can relate to not looking forward to your day to day lives and as a consequence your physical health suffers. As you can see, how you feel emotionally also plays a large role in determining how you feel physically.

If this passage hits home for you it is quite possible you need to evaluate your attitude and your current life circumstances. To be in a place of persistent displeasure makes it almost impossible to attain health and happiness. At times all that is required is an attitude adjustment while other times a complete lifestyle overhaul may be necessary. It is always important to focus on the good things in one's life and have gratitude for what you have. This shift in perspective to the positive may be enough to help you enjoy life thoroughly again. Other times for whatever reason, your career, relationships, and lifestyle may contradict with your inner nature. In these cases serious changes will be needed to regain balance and health.

Up to this point I have been speaking about general wellbeing and avoiding minor ailments. I will now touch briefly on major illness and the effect your thoughts have on manifesting them. I understand that diseases such as cancer are a sensitive topic for many people and I do not wish to oversimplify the cause of such an unfortunate occurrence.

Although the causes of life threatening disease are many and often appear inexplicable, I do wish to stress the point that our emotions and spiritual wellbeing directly tie into our physical wellbeing. Anger, resentment, sadness, depression, and jealousy all adversely affect our bodies in both the long and short term. Just think of how you feel when you get really angry. You probably get hot, your breath shortens, your pulse rises, and you may feel nauseous or dizzy. There is obviously a physical reaction to your emotional displeasure.

With this in mind now think about the accumulation of a lifetime of anger, jealousy, or sadness. If your body can be changed so dramatically from one incident imagine the long term effect of hundreds or thousands of similar incidents. You can think of these short or prolonged negative emotional states as having the effect of very slow acting poison. If gone untreated the long term result can be devastating.

Again I do not wish to imply that if you frequently get angry you will inevitably have to deal with a life threatening illness or vice versa. The point is that negative emotion does yield physical consequences. Western medicine is just starting to recognize the mind body connection in regards to health. We do not and probably will not fully know the consequence to perpetually living with strong negative emotion. For that reason it is imperative to keep those emotions in check and deal with them in an appropriate fashion.

With honest evaluation I am sure that most individuals will see that the way they think, act, and feel emotionally determines in large part how they feel physically. We cannot control a lot of things when it comes to our health but we can decide to live in gratitude. Once this shift in perspective occurs better health and overall wellbeing are sure to follow.

The exercises for this chapter are designed to help change the way you think. The more positive your thoughts and actions the better you will feel. Practice these exercises and you will notice a change for the better in the way you feel.

Exercise 1
"Attitude of Gratitude"

How often do you really stop and think about all of the great things in your life? If you are like most people you probably focus more on what you don't like about your life than what you do. This simple but profound exercise will help to change that focus. Each morning for at least 2 weeks sit down and write a list of all the things in your life that you are grateful for. It could be relationships, possessions, personality traits, career or anything else. Spend some time to really reflect and put it all down on paper. Your list may stay relatively the same each day or it may change and grow the longer you do it. Either way you will be making a conscious effort to put the good in your life at the forefront of your attention. Notice the changes that occur within you the longer you practice it. Hopefully it will become something that you will fit into your daily routine from now on. Again your attitude and outlook on life will have a large impact on your overall health; so decide to live in gratitude.

Exercise 2
"Life Evaluation"

You should now be able to see clearly that there is a lot in your life to be happy about. Now it's time to look at the things which deplete you and do not add joy to your experience. This is not an exercise in pessimistic reflection, rather an honest look at where and how you can change in order to attain lasting happiness and health. Write down all the ways in which you are not satisfied with your current life circumstances. The list could include finances, relationships, career, and environment, anything that you are not excited about. After writing it all down make an honest evaluation of what things are just you having a bad attitude and what needs to change or be eliminated. Many times after writing things down and thinking about them you will see that your complaints are silly or unwarranted. Other things like a constantly turbulent relationship, job that you hate, or unhealthy living environment may require action. Again if certain areas of your life fight against the person you truly are you will not be able to find peace and it is best to let them go. Hopefully the previous work you have done will allow you to easily differentiate between a major source of negativity and a trivial complaint. Once you have determined what needs to change do what needs to be done to change it. As those major stressors are eliminated from your life your health and joy will soar.

Exercise 3
"Think Healthy"

This exercise uses the power of affirmation. Simply tell yourself each morning and whenever you think of it throughout the day that you are healthy. You could say, "I enjoy perfect health each day," or "My body mind and spirit are in perfect balance." Anything to indicate to your consciousness that you desire health will work. In time you will naturally believe that you are healthy and your overall wellbeing will improve.

8

FIND AND DO WHAT
WORKS FOR YOU

How many of you have done certain things repeatedly even though they did not work for you? You try again and again without success and curse your bad luck or lack of ability. Why not try a new method rather than cursing the ineffective one? We waste so much energy doing things which don't suit our abilities and wonder why the results are not satisfactory. At this point you should have a solid grasp on who you are and this chapter will help you to see the benefit of utilizing your personal strengths.

By now you may realize that there is no benefit to being someone that you are not. What works for someone else will not necessarily work for you. Your job is to figure out how to most effectively live your life. It will most likely involve some trial and error, but the better you know yourself the easier it will be to implement strategies to make your life flow more efficiently.

I will first give examples to those of you still in school. Study habits and being successful in school in general can look very different depending on what works best for you. Again what is taught to be the traditional effective habits may or may not work for you. There are several different learning styles and if you determine which is best for you, you can save yourself a lot of time, stress, and energy.

In observing peers over the years I noticed that school, tests, and studying were a source of great anxiety for many. Some people would unnecessarily spend hours going over information they already knew. Others stressed out, did nothing, and were always unprepared. You must discover how you best absorb information and from there success in school should be much less difficult.

If you are someone who can easily retain information that is spoken to you that is great. Have confidence in this ability and don't waste time and energy, reading, rereading, and taking endless notes. You are lucky that you do not have to go to extreme measures to remember and regurgitate information. Remember that it is just as silly to do too much studying as it is to do none. In fact by over studying and worrying ceaselessly about knowing everything you are lessening your natural ability to succeed.

Other people find it difficult to retain a spoken lecture but can remember what they read very well. In this case your time and energy should be spent reading the text and your notes. Again having confidence in this talent should alleviate your stress and allow you to do well with less effort.

On the other end of the spectrum if it is difficult for you to absorb information in general, than a more disciplined approach to studying may be necessary. The combination of paying close attention in class, reading all the material, taking detailed notes and reviewing regularly should do the trick. In most cases what inhibits a person's ability to do well in school is a lack of confidence in one form or another. The more you tell yourself that you will be successful the more likely that you will be.

Hopefully this will lay groundwork for what I mean by finding and doing what works best. As you can imagine when you are best using your talents you can spend less time worrying and more time enjoying yourself. In general the more at ease you are, the more likely you are to succeed.

Here's another simple example which applies to me and many others. If you are someone who tends to get caught up in the flow of your day, and consequently things slip your mind, write things down. You could do it the old fashioned way or utilize the alarms, reminders and calendars which our cell phones are equipped with these days. This easy step can save you endless frustration and apologies. This chapter is all about making your life easier; so write it down and relax.

Many of us don't play to our strengths in our professional lives either. We do things which do not cater to our strengths and as a result we are not as productive as we could be. For example if you are great at networking and meeting people but are stuck doing paperwork half the time, this is not a good use of your talents. The same can be said if you are great at administrative duties but are forced to work in customer service. If you have a good understanding of what you do best then make every effort to stick to what works. Understandably you can't always control what you are asked to do at work, but showcase your talents and hopefully your success will speak for itself.

In short it is difficult to find success and happiness in your career if you do not do the things which work best. Staying in a career which does not suit you simply because you were offered the job, will lead to burn out and dissatisfaction over time. Everyone has unique talents which bring about joy and fulfillment, so figure out what they are and display them as often as you can.

Another major area where we do not do what works best is in how we nourish our bodies. How many of you can actually say you feel energized and uplifted after every meal. I'm guessing that many actually feel worse after they eat than they did before. I know that has been the case for me at times.

The reason for this is simple; we rarely give our bodies what works best for them. We eat whatever is most convenient, which usually means pre-made and processed food which lacks the key nutrients our body needs to operate efficiently. The result of careless eating is poor health, lack of energy, depressed mood, lack of motivation etc., etc. We each have total control over what goes into our mouths each day so why not choose the things which make us feel better.

This again is not a one size fits all process. Some people require more carbohydrates to stay energized; others need a lot of protein. This is relatively easy to figure out by slowly adjusting your diet until you notice yourself feeling good after eating, rather than lethargic and sluggish. In general we can all benefit by eating more fruits and vegetables and less refined sugar and artificial ingredients. I can assure you that once you figure out a diet that works best for you, you will not want to go back to the days of pop tarts and fast foods on a regular basis.

The ways which you can best utilize your unique make-up are endless. In time you will start to intuitively do what works best. The more you start to get to know yourself and analyze what isn't working for you the closer you are to finding what does. Remember that the process outlined in this book is personal, so try not to let the success of someone else influence your growth. Ultimately each of us should be the best judge of ourselves when it comes to finding what works best in our lives.

Here again are some exercises that should help to show you your unique gifts and how to use them.

Exercise 1
Take Inventory

We all have strengths and weaknesses. This exercise is about identifying them so as to best utilize them. The first part of the process is simple. In two columns write down the things you love to do, and the things that you are best at. This could be aspects of your personality, activities which you enjoy, or anything you feel is a natural talent of yours. In the other column write down the opposite which include the things you really do not like doing or that you consider weaknesses. Be as honest and detailed as possible. After you have compiled both lists it is time to do some introspection and more writing. In your own way write down your thoughts and feelings about how your strengths and weaknesses show up in your life. Also include ways in which you think you could put more energy towards your strengths and less towards your weaknesses. For example acknowledge all the things you do that cater to your natural abilities. Also notice all the time you spend doing things that you don't enjoy or do not have a natural inclination toward. If you are unfulfilled with your career add a list of careers that suit what you do best or love to do. This is really an exercise in self-evaluation. The goal is to put down on paper what is and is not working for you at this time in your life. Hopefully after seeing it all you will be able to keep what is helping you and adjust what is not. I bet you will be surprised at what comes out of this process once you start.

Exercise 2
You Are What You Eat

As I mentioned many of us do not pay enough attention to what we eat. This exercise is not a diet but rather a way to gradually change your eating habits permanently. To start, I suggest that you adjust 2 meals per week. First instead of having chips or fried food with your lunch or dinner replace it with a salad or vegetable. Next replace 1 dessert with fruit. Try to notice the difference in how you feel after your meal with the replacement as opposed to what you would have normally chosen. The difference should be apparent and hopefully will lead to a gradual shift to healthier choices. Also try different options and experiment to see what combination of foods makes you feel the best.

Exercise 3
If It's Broke Fix It

As I mentioned, many of us get into patterns of behavior even though the results are not satisfactory. We do things again and again out of habit whether or not they are truly working for us. This exercise is designed to get out of those unproductive ruts. Basically if you feel stagnant or that your routine is not helping you anymore, change it! It could be as simple as switching the order you do things in the morning, or taking an alternate route to work. You will be surprised how a small adjustment can make a big difference. It is easy to get caught up in our day to day lives and essentially put it on autopilot. These little tweaks should get you out of your robotic trance and let you see that there are other ways to get your responsibilities accomplished. Ideally by making some minor adjustments you will find a routine that works better for you. If nothing else you will get a slightly different perspective on your day which is always a good thing.

9

OPEN NEW DOORS
WITHOUT SHUTTING
OLD ONES

Have you ever acted in the heat of the moment and later regretted it? So often we make decisions when our judgment is affected by strong emotion. Do you ever wish you could have some of those moments back? Unfortunately we all know that we cannot change the actions we have taken in the past. All we can hope to do is change our patterns of behavior so that we do not repeat our mistakes.

This chapter will hopefully give you the insight needed to keep a steady flow of new opportunity coming without burning bridges along the way. We never know when a friend or job reference will be able to help us in the future so it is best to keep positive relationships whenever possible. I do not wish to imply that we should be disingenuous with people on the chance that they will do us a favor in the future. Instead I am saying that it is a good practice to keep one's options open regarding people and circumstances because you never know when one or both will be good for you at a later date.

In general nurturing every relationship that comes into your life is a good idea. I have identified 4 main areas where many of us let emotion get the best of us and as a result we waste energy and opportunity for future benefit. These are the relationships we have with friends, family, romantic partners, and employers. Resentments and grudges over perceived injustice are damaging to one's mind body, and soul. Wouldn't you rather clear the air and move on instead of letting past events weigh you down and affect your present and future? It is so common in our society to cut ties with people abruptly, that we do not realize the harmful effects these unresolved disputes have on us. In most cases arguments can be resolved and you can move on to new things without having to shut the door on your past.

Although the lesson is essentially the same for all types of relationships, let's first discuss friendships. Many of us can relate to a betrayal of some kind by someone you considered to be a friend. We felt wronged, and those hurt feelings translated into an immediate and possibly ugly end to what had previously been a rich friendship. At times betrayal by a friend can feel like the worst kind. I am not saying that you should somehow not allow actions of your friends to hurt you. Our aim is to work on our reaction and decide whether or not the result of that reaction is what you truly want.

Depending on the exact circumstances the friendship may or may not have to end. What is more important is the way that it ends. To blow up and immediately turn your back on the person will most likely have lingering negative effects on any future friendships. It is very important to communicate after the initial pain has subsided. Let your feelings be known in a calm and clear way. In some cases there are unknown misunderstandings about the situation which would not have been brought to light without this nonthreatening conversation. Other times it may simply be a forum for you to be heard and from there move on without lingering consequences.

Only you can decide what the best course is to take after this conversation has taken place. The important aspect is that you give yourself and the other person a chance to clear the air. This interaction can bring about a resolution which allows the friendship to continue. If not, the goal is to leave without holding onto any feelings of resentment or hatred. Again keeping these negative feelings is never beneficial and only lessens the chances of having successful relationships in the future. Remember that to be hurt by a friend is bad enough; do not let that pain stay with you any longer than it needs to.

Much like friendships, our romantic relationships have the potential to bring up pain and hurt feelings. We generally invest a lot of time and energy into the relationships we have with our partners. In turn any perceived wrongdoing could easily sting the most. Here again the goal is not to salvage a relationship that has been damaged beyond repair. What we want to avoid is a heat of the moment separation wherein the end comes without any definitive closure. When we end a romantic partnership too abruptly we don't give ourselves a chance to heal and move on. Somewhere in our consciousness we are left with unresolved feelings of betrayal which carry over to any and all future attempts at successful partnerships.

On the other hand, if we allow the initial emotion to dissipate and make a decision from that place, a healthy breakup is possible. Once again it is vital that we voice our feelings in a calm and civil way so that the other person does not respond with defensiveness or hostility. In order to have closure, both parties need to be able to express how they feel and be heard. When you interact in this way you leave open the possibility of reconciliation. If you both effectively communicate your side, you should feel much lighter when the conversation is complete. At that point the decision to move on or stay together is made under the proper pretenses.

As with any type of close relationship, grudges with family members can happen quickly and cause prolonged pain and suffering. You probably have experienced or know someone who has experienced a falling out with a family member. Tempers flare on both sides and the egos of each will not allow the situation to be forgiven. Once again a lifelong relationship is cut off because of something that will most likely seem insignificant over time.

The solution to this scenario is much the same as with the others I have mentioned. Wait for your anger and emotion to dissipate and then attempt to speak openly with the other party. Admit fault if appropriate for your part in things and most likely your family member will do the same. We come into this world with certain family members for a reason, so I cannot think of too many situations that could warrant the complete dismissal of someone that you know and love. Save yourself possibly years of discomfort by talking it out as soon as you feel ready.

Your career life is the last area in which I will discuss the value of keeping doors open. Many of us can relate to being laid off or being put in a situation at work where we felt it was necessary to quit. The question is how did you react to those situations in the moment? If you are like me it is quite possible that you let your emotions get the best of you and you slammed the door shut on any future working relationship.

In cases where you feel wronged in the workplace it is not always possible to honestly discuss what happened and why. What you can always do is keep your reaction civilized and do what you can to let go of any ill will you may have about the situation. It is natural to feel that you deserve an explanation, but often it will be in your best interest to simply accept what has happened and move forward. By holding onto that feeling of needing answers you will be hindering your ability to receive the next opportunity which is inevitably coming your way.

This brings me to the flip side of this chapter, the opening of new doors. I have stressed the importance of keeping your personal relationships (doors) open. The natural result of doing this is that you will allow new people and opportunities to come into your life more freely. Again it is much harder to attract new relationships or circumstances when you are agonizing over the ones from your past. The point is not to keep people in your life who are no longer good for you, but rather bring freeing closure to those relationships which aren't working in order to make room for new ones that will.

Exercise 1
Did I do that?

Have you ever asked yourself that question? This exercise is all about being honest with yourself and recognizing the times when your hasty reactions may not have been the best ones. Simply think back and write down those times when you acted out of anger and burned bridges or shut doors as a result. Was it a family feud, a heated argument with a partner, or a grudge with a friend? List everything you can think of and describe the situation. What we are trying to learn from this is that we may act in this way more often than we think. Ideally it will give you some insight and awareness into your behavior patterns so that you can act differently in the future.

Exercise 2
It's my Fault

No one likes to admit that they are wrong or say they are sorry. In a heated argument we want to focus on what the other person did to upset us and not what we may have done to provoke it. In this practice you will actively take responsibility for your side of things. It takes 2 to tango in a disagreement, so rather than place blame on someone else, try apologizing for what you did to help create the situation. Very simply the next time you get in an argument which ends unresolved, be the one to initiate reconciliation. After the dust has settled and you can speak calmly, seek out the person and admit your part in what happened. Most likely it will lead to the other person doing the same, but if not at least you have made the effort to repair things.

This practice if done with pure intentions should lead to a large decrease in shutting doors unnecessarily.

Exercise 3
Get Real

Many of you have already had an instance or more in your life where an event has caused a complete cutting of ties with someone you were once close to. This exercise is designed for those cases. Here we want to take an honest look back at whatever it was that caused communication to stop. Try to recall what happened, who was involved and why you were hurt so badly. After that evaluate the time since the event occurred, and what was lost or gained as a result, whether you still feel the pain or for how long you actually did. Basically try to determine if the decision to cut ties was the right one then, and if it remains the right one now. My guess is that in most cases you have wasted at least some time and energy unnecessarily on this grudge. If so take the appropriate steps to make it better. If you do determine your decision was the right one then you should not feel like the issue remains unresolved. This process should give you the closure you need or the realization that you should try to repair that relationship.

10

FIND YOUR PURPOSE

Do you wake up each day excited and feeling like you are living the life you are meant to live? If not, why? It is every human being's right to the life which they desire. Each of us is born with unique gifts that if shared will allow us to be of optimal service to mankind. I have mentioned throughout this book everyone can and should be true to themselves and never settle for a life which is not suited to their nature. This chapter will hammer home the importance of living a life on purpose and with purpose.

The work you have done thus far has likely given you a clearer picture of the real you. In most cases you have realized that you have sold yourself short and wasted a lot of time and energy along the way. In addition my hope is that you have been shown who you want to be and are most definitely capable of becoming. All of this work has led to your life mission which is to find and achieve your purpose.

By studying the lives of the most influential and successful people in history you would find at least a couple of common threads. The first, which is the key to any and all lasting happiness and success, is the drive towards fulfilling their purpose. All of those people had a clear vision of, and unrelenting motivation towards, achieving whatever it was they had their sights on. Despite any obstacles or circumstances which may have appeared to be failures, they pushed forward until the life that they desired was theirs.

Another common theme amongst these individuals was awareness that they must consider the greater good in their pursuits. All of them left a positive and enduring impression upon the world which we now share. I do not want to mistake monetary wealth for the success and purpose that I am referring to. The world has plenty of people willing to do anything for extreme wealth. The problem is that although this goal can be achieved, it alone does not come with it the happiness and fulfillment that accompany benefiting mankind.

Just look at the many entertainers and or entrepreneurs who have achieved fame and fortune only to wind up miserable and unfulfilled. What these individuals did not realize is that money can buy fun for a while, but unless the goal is extended to the amount of good that can be done with that wealth and fame they will never be satisfied. The unique gifts I mentioned are designed to be a pathway towards bringing joy and positivity to the world no matter how big or small the scale.

Some may make the mistake of thinking that unless you are the president, or rich and famous, that you cannot have a significant impact on the world. The truth is that although living out your purpose can bring with it wealth and high levels of recognition, it is not necessary. Many of the most significant contributors to the greater good are not known outside of their friends and family. Have you ever had a teacher who inspired you to be a better person? Have you ever had a doctor who made you feel like your wellbeing was their only concern? Have you ever been blown away by the great service you received from a waitress? If you answered yes to any of those questions it is most likely that those people are unknown to almost everyone on Earth. Even so, I guarantee that they are happy and know that they are on the right path.

Your purpose very well could be to give your children the best childhood possible. It may sound like a small feat, but if accomplished you have fulfilled your reason for living which is the greatest gift you can give to mankind. Never go against the voice inside you which is trying to tell you what your purpose is. It is important that you do not get caught in the trap of doing what your friends or family think you should do. It comes back to accepting their advice as coming from a good place, but believing you know best how your life should unfold.

Once you have done the internal work necessary to find out who you are and who you want to be your purpose should reveal itself. When you know what that purpose is, your job is to make sure each day you are moving towards it. This does not mean that after reading this book and discovering your purpose that you will instantly be able to achieve it. In fact you will no doubt encounter obstacles that may make it seem like your goal is unattainable. Remember that nothing done with purpose is unattainable and that all the struggles you push through are only designed to prepare you for your desired end.

As I said every great innovator, leader, and philosopher in history faced seemingly insurmountable odds to get where they are in our minds. They knew that each road block was a blessing to show them a better way of doing what they were supposed to do. Failure is only true failure if you give up. Otherwise it is a lesson learned and a mistake never to repeat.

It is important to remember that the way you make your living will not always directly relate to your ultimate purpose. If this is the case you must always keep your focus on that ultimate goal. The circumstances will align themselves in your favor as long as you do not waiver from what you believe is your purpose. Do what you can each day to make it a reality and eventually it will be no matter how far off it seems today.

The vast majority of people alive today are suffering in some way in large part due to the fact that they ignore their true calling. Fear, ego, laziness, complacency all overpower their ability to find and live out their purpose. I can say with certainty that everyone is equally capable of living their purpose. Until you are, it is impossible to achieve the everlasting happiness and contentment which we are all searching for. Also part of living your purpose is the journey which gets you there. Enjoy all the minor events on your way to your ultimate achievement. In this way you can have that happiness all along if you keep in mind that all your work is necessary for your desired end to come to fruition. Remember that by living out your purpose you are doing everything you can to improve our world as a whole.

I hope this has given you the inspiration and drive needed to create the life you were meant to live. The 3 exercises that follow are very strong suggestions. They will help you to find and achieve your purpose in life.

Exercise 1
Define Your Purpose

It is vital that you have a clear vision of what you hope to accomplish in living out your purpose. For this reason this exercise asks you to define it. Simply write down exactly what it is that you feel is your ultimate purpose in life. What do you want to do? Who do you want to help? Take significant time with this process because it could lead to your lifelong path. Be truly introspective and dedicate the care necessary to create an exact definition of your individual purpose. The more work you have done thus far the easier this should be. Take your time and I'm sure you will create something perfect for you.

Exercise 2
Make a Plan

After you have the exact picture of what you want to do you must determine how you are going to do it. Every desired outcome has a series of events which will lead to its realization. It is very important that you create a precise road map as to how you are going to reach your goal. If you know someone who has done or is doing what you want to do, utilize their experience to draw up your plans. Without clear direction it is unlikely you will succeed and very likely you will give up due to frustration. This is a similar process to creating the definition. The answers will come as you become more attuned to your inner workings. Once you have the plan in place start work on it right away. Do what you can each day to move closer to that final step.

Exercise 3
Too Legit to Quit

This exercise is both the easiest and the hardest. It is simple. NEVER GIVE UP. Your purpose is too legit to quit! No matter what obstacles are put in your path, work through them and you will see that they were necessary and helpful in the end. See each temporary failure as fuel to your fire and soon those obstacles will melt away. If accomplishing your ultimate life goal was easy, everyone would do it. Be one of the select few who cannot be stopped in their pursuit of true purpose and happiness in life. Happy trails.

PART 3
STAYING ON TRACK

This journey has finally come back full circle. The energy and inspiration that drove the beginning stages of this book have returned in a more subtle and focused manner. As I mentioned early on, the motivation and determination to start and finish this work hit me suddenly with the force of a lightning bolt. All at once I was seeing the life of my dreams unfold before my eyes. I knew with undeniable certainty who I was and where I was going.

As I have described in detail, the certainty of those few weeks was shaken in a profound way which led to the series of events that have been my life since. Although the plan I had for myself did not come to fruition, I know that everything that did occur was and will continue to be necessary for my growth and development. The years since I first sat down to start this project have given me life experience and deeper understanding of the lessons I am trying to teach. I would not trade any of the pain or struggle I went through because I am confident that those are the parts of my life which will allow me to most help my fellow man.

I do believe that if I had lived my life according to the steps I laid out, I could have avoided many difficulties. That being said, those difficulties returned me to that same wisdom eventually and to a life at this moment I do not want to ever lose.

I feel it is necessary to sum up the most recent happenings of this journey to illustrate how it all came back to living by the 10 lessons I was so passionate about all those years ago. As is always the case, the truth is the greatest liberator we can pursue. Living by the truth of who we are and want to be allows an infinite number of possibilities and opportunities to open.

Being true to myself after many years of self-delusion was what brought me back to the path I intended to walk all along. Something I did not mention about my time on Martha's Vineyard was a brief yet very powerful interaction with the woman who is now my wife. Even though our meeting was brief and limited, the feelings which are still the purest I have ever known were cultivated from that point.

This brings me years ahead to the time when I was deciding to stay or leave Los Angeles. Following my truth had enabled me to end a relationship which was not working anymore, and now I was faced with needing to know if this person on the Vineyard and I were meant to be together as I suspected. Thanks to the wondrous World Wide Web and specifically Facebook, I was able to contact the person.

Once I knew the possibility was there to form a relationship I wasted little time making plans to return to Martha's Vineyard. I did not make it known initially that my intentions for going there were to see if my feelings were correct. All I really said was that circumstances lead me to move back and I would see her soon. The trip itself also spawned from my being true to what I needed at that time. Driving across the country alone without any definitive prospects waiting for me was a risky endeavor. I knew that, but I also knew that I would regret not doing it in the manner which felt right to me. I of course was met with some doubt and skepticism from people whose opinions I value. Even so my heart was telling me that I was right and as I have always found to be the case, my heart knew what was best for me.

The point being I was able to tap into my inner nature or truth and from that place I was given the path I needed. All of this ties in nicely to my second lesson involving the use of intuition rather than fear for guidance. In my opinion if I didn't do anything that I had some level of fear about, I would do very little and be rather unfulfilled.

Of course I was afraid to leave a place that had provided me with so many positives. I had friends, experience in a field that is in demand, and the comfort of being surrounded by people who were on similar paths. Leaving all of that supplied me with plenty of fear but the method of travel and destination only compounded it. I would travel alone for weeks and 95% of the trip was in locations I had never visited. Also I was returning to a place where I had gone through some of the lowest points in my life. Not to mention I was doing all of it for a love that I had no way of knowing would be returned.

I could easily have listened to the fears and doubts I had and talked myself out of it. Luckily I listened to the thoughts that made me feel good rather than the ones that made me feel uneasy, and ultimately made the right choice for me. I am not saying that it is always easy to determine whether or not an idea is a good one. My experience is that if you quiet yourself and the idea still resonates with you, then the fear associated with it is not legitimate.

After I let go of the fear that came with leaving Los Angeles, I immediately was able to find the abundance of beauty around me. Throughout my cross country drive natural beauty revived my mind body and spirit. I witnessed amazing sunsets and sunrises, drove through vast desert land, and saw miles of lush green pastures. It was truly a gift to reconnect with nature during those weeks of driving and reflection.

Even after I reached my destination I had a renewed appreciation for the beauty of the island. I spent more time at the beaches which I had previously taken for granted. I also reconnected with my love of hiking and found many incredible trails which I didn't know existed. I have definitely found since leaving LA that the beauty of nature can and does provide me with an abundance of positive energy.

As I said earlier, I came back to Martha's Vineyard in order to re-unite with my (now) wife which involves the physical aspect of beauty. I can honestly say that she is my dream come true in every way including physically. Obviously being married to a woman to whom I am so strongly attracted is yet another constant source of energy that I have at my disposal.

More importantly she and others I have met in my recent past provide me with the creative and intellectual beauty that I crave as well. We happen to share many beliefs and philosophies on life and sharing ideas and feelings with her and my other close friends allows me to find peace and confidence in another way.

Last but not least the creative beauty that now surrounds me fulfills all of the requirements. My wife is an amazing singer and writer. Every time I get to hear her I am inspired. There are also many other artists, musicians and writers on the Vineyard from whom I receive inspiration and energy. By being true to myself, and ignoring fear, I have restored limitless amounts of beauty to my life.

In addition to the abundance of natural beauty that I encountered on my drive cross country, I was also given ample time for myself. It occurs to me now that even after stopping the reckless and unhealthy lifestyle; I still had not taken any time for myself. For the first year and a half I was in treatment at a 15 person recovery house. After that I jumped immediately into a committed and somewhat restrictive relationship. Neither of these living situations allowed for any significant "me" time.

My journey back to Martha's Vineyard was in part so appealing for just that reason. I was traveling by myself and under no strict time line or schedule. After living for 3 and half years under what felt like constant surveillance, this was just what I needed. It was quite refreshing to be free from any ties or outside distractions. I really enjoyed my time driving, resting, meditating, writing and exploring different cities by myself. It gave me a chance to reflect and recharge which I sorely needed.

I am not saying that most people need to take weeks by themselves in order to recharge. I was fortunate to have that opportunity, but the key is to recognize when you are lacking sufficient alone time in your day to day life. Since reaching the island I have not stayed in seclusion to keep my peace of mind. What I have done is brought balance back into my life.

I no longer feel drained because someone needs to know where I am and what I am doing all the time. For me, some meditation, reading, writing, or a short walk is all that I now need to be refreshed and better suited for productive joyful days. I am grateful that I was given the chance to travel myself in order to remember this. I had not given myself that chance in a long time. It reminded me why I felt taking time for one's self was so important all those years ago.

My recent history also required that I accept other's beliefs while keeping my own. This lesson closely relates to letting go of fear and following intuition. As I mentioned there were those who told me it was not a good idea to leave LA without any real plan or solid prospects. It was easy for me to see where they were coming from, and it's possible that had the roles been reversed I would have had the same doubts for someone else. I didn't get mad at the fact that my friends had concerns. I knew that they were telling me their honest opinion about the situation.

Although I could see that what they were saying had validity, I did not let it change my belief of what I felt was best for me. The same was true when I decided to propose to my wife after only dating for a few months. I was aware that the news would be shocking and of concern to some of my family. Again I could put myself in their shoes to see where they were coming from. It was not necessary for me to argue or get angry that they were not as sure as I was about the decision. I accepted their belief but made my choice based on my own beliefs. When you are in touch with your intuition there is no need to be defensive or hostile when you face differences of opinion. The right answers are always inside you if you are attuned to them. Seeing someone else's perspective is not the same as adopting that perspective. Know that most people give opinions and advice with good intentions, but that does not mean they know better than you what is best.

After accepting others beliefs, I have again tried to encourage others beliefs. This is something I have always tried to do but more so recently. When talking about encouraging others I am mostly referring to people's aspirations and dreams. I am a strong believer that everyone should follow their highest aspirations in life.

Whenever I talk to someone about what they want to do with their lives I always encourage them to pursue the biggest dream they have. Most recently I have encouraged my wife's goals of becoming a successful singer, writer and humanitarian. Also whenever a friend tells me they want to travel or take a risk towards a life goal, I never hesitate to push them in that direction. The main point of this book is to show people that the life of their wildest dreams is attainable, and I take great pleasure in reinforcing that fact to anyone I can.

I believe that achieving goals is helped along by the power of suggestion and the thoughts you have about any desired outcome. That relates nicely with the next lesson. It is amazing to me but I have even been given another example of how sickness is a mental manifestation in my recent history. While I was driving across the country the panic over the swine flu was just beginning. Not only that, but I was driving in an area of the country that was reporting a majority of the early cases. Every day I felt bombarded with stories about this life threatening flu. In addition, I was changing climate essentially every other day which for many can become a cause for illness. To top it all off the journey itself could very easily have become a source of major stress on my mind and body. Despite all of those factors working against me I felt quite well the entire trip, even better than I had in many years.

I am very confident that I felt so great because I was following the path that I was meant to be on. I wasn't affected by the stress or risk of flu because I felt overwhelmingly positive about the decisions I was making. Of course there is a flip side to this lesson which became a reality a few months down the road.

After a few months I did end up contracting the swine flu. The main difference then was that I was feeling huge amounts of resentment, anger, and hostility towards someone who was intentionally trying to be disruptive in the lives of my wife and me. I had never been consumed by such overwhelming negativity in my life, and as a result I became more physically ill than I ever had before.

I have no doubt that both were closely related because I had been around many people with the virus prior to those negative emotions taking over my thoughts. Also my wife who was living with me did not contract the flu. To me this proves that we all have a choice when it comes to physical ailments. Had I not let anger overcome me as it did I know that my body's defenses would have protected me from any virus. I say this based on personal experience and the fact that I had not had anything worse than a runny nose in close to 15 years. Subconscious desire for sickness and negative emotion are far more toxic to the body than merely coming in contact with a cold or flu. All people are more or less exposed to the same germs and bacteria every day, yet some stay healthy and some do not. The difference lies not in the physical but the emotional and spiritual realm.

In order to stay in balance and minimize stress it is important to find and do what works for you. For all those years I neglected what brought me joy and confidence and replaced it with activities revolved around drinking and drug use. Even though I thought I was doing what worked for me, the events in my life and the way I felt most of the time proved that I was not.

My life since has been a slow adjustment back to the things which really do work. They include maintaining a healthy lifestyle of regular physical activity and nutritious eating. I still receive peace and happiness from playing sports either competitively or for fun. Healthier eating habits are a new addition to my lifestyle which has proven to be just as beneficial to my overall wellbeing.

Again daily reflection and meditation also work in my life to bring balance and perspective. Similarly I read literature which inspires me and resonates with my true nature. Journaling or any free form writing also work to calm me down and release built up stress.

In regards to how I interact with people it has remained much the same. I often try to make light of situations and be friendly with anyone I meet. I also like to listen to others when they have difficulties in their life which very often results in people trusting me quickly.

One last thing I do which has always worked for me is to be generous in all areas of my life. Some might not see the significance but I tip well to all people working in service positions. Also whenever I have some extra money I give to charitable organizations which I feel strongly about. Possibly more importantly than giving money I also make an effort to be generous with my time. It could be giving a ride, helping someone move, or just sitting with someone who needs an ear. In my experience all forms of generosity are beneficial to both the giver and receiver. I truly believe that it is one way of living that will work wonders for anyone and everyone.

My latest example of how to open new doors without shutting old ones came as a huge shock to me. In short since the last time that I sat down to write, my wife and I decided to separate. Initially my thoughts were that my whole journey back to the Vineyard and most of what I had written about was meaningless. In my mind if the person I thought I was going to spend the rest of my life with was not that person, then it must mean that it was all for nothing.

Amazingly in a very short period of time I was able to see that that was not the case. The two of us had a very honest and open talk about what was going on between us. We both agreed that at the time we were not capable of being in a healthy marriage. Although we still loved and cared for each other immensely, we needed time to figure some things out individually before we could hope to succeed in a relationship with anyone else.

Neither of us regrets what we did. We got married because we were in love and that is what our hearts told us to do. We did not foresee it ending this way but understood that it was for the best. Somehow after having this very real and emotional talk we were joking and making each other laugh within minutes.

Now because we didn't allow anger and negativity to take over we have kept a door open. We both see that we came into each other's lives for a reason. Since we were able to part ways peacefully, the possibility of reconciliation was there. Whether or not we get back together is not important. The important factor is that we can move on without destroying any sort of possible relationship in the future.

The whole experience confused me. I never expected to leave my wife, much less leave and be on great terms. I am very confident that this was even possible because of the internal work I have done and the inner understanding that I have. I do not mean to imply that my experience with a marriage ending is easy to accomplish or even the best in all circumstances. I am just glad that I am able to move forward towards new doors knowing that I have not shut any behind me. (We have since gotten back together and have a beautiful son.)

Everything that happened in my recent life brought me back to what this book is ultimately about. Fortunately for me my purpose has remained the same over all this time and throughout all the ups and downs. I started this book with the hope that it could help people see that the life they dream of is within their grasp. I hope to inspire and teach my fellow men and women how to be the persons they were born to be.

Another event in my life gave me that final nudge I needed to make this dream I have had for so long into reality. Only about a month before my wife and I decided to separate, I was hit by a car from behind which was traveling roughly 40 miles per hour. From all accounts I was very lucky to survive and to suffer only a major leg and knee injury. The accident opened my eyes to the fact that I had let fear and doubt prevent me from fully committing myself to the life that I desire. I realized that although I have always known that life is very precious, I have not always lived in a way that coincides with that belief.

I clearly saw that I was given this life for a reason, but I have been the only one standing in the way of achieving that reason. A friend of mine talked to me shortly after the accident and said that this would be my time to find my passion. He was not aware of this book or that I already knew what that passion was. It was yet another sign that I needed to do what I had wanted to do for so long. I reclaimed my purpose and hope that it will spark the purposes of countless others. This has been an incredible journey which has led me back to my original purpose for writing this book. Thank you to all who have shared in this process with me and may you live each day as the man or woman you are meant to be.

PART 4
ENDING AT THE BEGINNING

1

THE TRUTH IS
LIBERATING

My parents relayed this relatively simple message onto me from a very young age. When you are young the truth is all you want to know, you want to know how things work, where babies come from, and why the sky is blue. Subconsciously you will take everything you are told as the truth. A question that intrigues children to this day is, "Is there a Santa Claus?" My honest belief is that if you believe with all your heart that there is, then that truth is your reality.

I remember being a child, and when Christmas time came around that day would occupy my thoughts almost constantly. I had no fear of homework, or yard work, or having people accept me. I was content to get excited about this day and nothing would distract me or bring me down until the day in fact arrived. This passion, I believe, had to do with the whole Christmas spirit along with the fact that I was born on Christmas day. Since my thoughts at that young and uncorrupted age were so clear and pure it is no wonder that I could not be brought down by any outside force from this wonderful excitement based high. What I realize today is that this principle of pure truth and intention can have the same effect at any age.

As the years past and I was able to come in contact with more people and learn others beliefs on the world, my thoughts and realities slowly began to change. This can bring me back to just one moment in my life that has in fact changed me ever since. While attending an after school gathering, at the age of probably six or seven, the topic of Santa Claus somehow was brought up. Almost immediately one person without hearing anyone else's opinion blurted out, "there is no Santa Claus." All of a sudden my reality was questioned and I was determined to see if this person's bluntness had in fact been the "truth."

As soon as I and my sister arrived home we sought out the consolation of my mother, for she was the only parent available at the time. We asked straight out, "is there a Santa Claus, and we want the truth." Instantly you could see an internal struggle, where she was faced with the decision of whether or not this magical innocent being was in fact in existence at the present time. Finally after some obvious internal debate she resolved to tell us the truth as honestly as she believed it.

Her honest reply was, "truthfully at this time, Santa Claus is not a reality, aside from what people make of it. Although this is true I strongly believe that there was in fact a real man from which the myth originated." All this was said to two children, both of ages below ten, but since the truth liberates you, we could not feel cheated or deceived. That was our perfect moment to learn the truth about a much debated topic.

This knowledge did change me but it did not instill in me a desire to make others believe what I already did. I knew that learning the truth was momentarily disappointing, but at the same time created a lifetime of liberation from a myth. Everyone needs to and does find this out at some point in their life, and for everyone it will be the exact moment that they are ready to hear it.

Another thing that I have noticed over the course of my relatively short lifetime is that as you get older time seems to go by much quicker. With age comes responsibility and as the responsibilities become greater it seems the time to get them done gets shorter. Nothing in fact could be further from the "truth." Reality is precisely what you make of it, and time is then just a frame of mind. The expression, "time flies when you're having fun," could not be simpler or more correct. When you are having a good time it seems effortless and therefore you want to stay in that state of minimal effort for as long as possible.

Take for instance recess at school, almost all school age children anticipate recess every day, and love every minute when they are participating in it. The time seems to be extremely short when in fact it is as long as or longer than most other academic portions of the day. It only seems shorter because you have the desire to be in that state of mind all the time. The "truth," which is that you want the whole day to be recess, is liberating when you are in fact in recess.

Wouldn't it be nice to always be in the frame of mind that what you are doing is exactly what you want to be doing at any given moment? I in fact am living this reality and that is why I am writing this book to let people realize that life CAN be recess all the time.

Throughout my adolescence and probably many others as well, I found myself making a conscious effort to be what everyone else thought I should be. It seemed as soon as I entered middle school, everything that I had known in elementary school was not the "truth" anymore. You needed brand name clothes, and to be funny, but not too smart. The popular kids were the ones, who in fact, probably were the least true to themselves. I admit to being somewhat a part of this problem. I did let people influence my decisions and did not stay true to what I knew worked best for me.

The more I tried to be someone that I wasn't the less happy I was. Even if I seemed to gain friends by outward appearance, I was in fact shutting out more people than I was letting in. The more I tried to be popular the less successful I was. This was purely due to the fact that I was not liberating myself by being true to myself. Every person is born with innocence and if everyone could keep that undefined quality for the rest of their lives the world would be in an infinitely different place than it is.

It was a constant struggle for me to get through middle school. Trying to live up to others expectations creates worlds of undue stress and mental blockages. I wanted so badly to be accepted by everyone, that I did everything except be myself. During these years I was very often sick and never felt truly awake and/or alive. Everything I knew was being covered up and jaded by what others thought to be the right way to do things. These years were truly the most trying in my short lifetime, but they helped me to grow and mature at exactly the right pace. I know now, that my life took that path for specific reasons, and I could not be sitting here writing this book had it not been for all that I have experienced. I have no ill will towards anyone who has tried to change me for I realize that they must have thought that they were right at the time. I wish to take something significant away from everyone and everything I meet or do.

Although these years were so tough, I believed always that things could only get better. I entered high school with a mix of excitement for a new start, along with apprehension that most feel when entering a new situation. I was confident that I had everything necessary to realize my goals both socially and academically. From the first day I saw that high school would be some of the most fun times of my life. Almost immediately, it seemed like I was in lunch and talking and relating to people that I never really took the time to converse with before. I liked this freedom of knowing people but not having them come with preconceptions. My liberating truth was that I could adapt to new situations and very quickly build strong connections with people I never even had thought about before.

Almost as soon as I entered high school I enjoyed living much more. It is such a different and more open minded environment, especially where I live, that you can't help but feel accepted by almost every-one you make an effort to talk to. Quickly my social place was moving up the ranks, I was not the most popular kid by any means, but I also had no desire to be. I was fairly content to be where I was, but I was still not being completely true to myself.

In class I was fairly quiet aside from the occasional one liner to get a reaction. I was very reserved and always thought before I spoke, so as not to make mistakes. I realize now that you have to make mistakes to make progress, just ask Thomas Edison. Nonetheless I was shy and not outspoken at all. If I had a question, I would wait for someone else to ask it, and if no one did, I would not do what I didn't know how to do. The truth comes when you realize that you have much more to gain from asking a question than you have from not asking it at all. Everyone has exactly the same right to learn and understand in school, and the people that take the risks and ask the relevant questions should be commended and will undoubtedly be the most successful.

With high school comes temptation and risks. All of which you have to analyze and decide for yourself whether or not you want to be a part of them. The first that I was faced with was alcohol. I thought and was told to think that everyone drinks and it's not bad etc. So one day I thought I would try and get drunk. My parents, although not drinkers themselves, for some reason did have a bottle of alcohol in the house. So being the bar tender I was at fourteen years old I made myself a nice vodka and orange juice. I don't really know how much I put in but of course I had to assume that if alcohol was in me I was in fact drunk. Well I let the good times roll at this point, I stumbled, tried to play basketball, and to tie my shoes. I am convinced today that I was not at all drunk but the mind can and does create false realities for you. If I had in fact gotten drunk, then telling the truth of the story would have been liberating, but the truth was I hadn't been, although that did not stop me from saying I was.

I made up a false transformation of the truth so as to have a better story and gain more respect from my peers. I realize now though that undue respect is worse than no respect at all. If people only want to be around you because of things you have made up to impress them then those relationships will never be close and will inevitably end up hurting both involved. If I had told the truth that I was not actually drunk, but I tried to be, I would have been much better off and not had to stress over how to make the story sound better.

Next along the course of high school evolution was the desire to try out the famous gateway drug maryjane, gangha, reefer, wacky tobacky, nuggets, etc. I wanted to try marijuana. So shortly after I gained the desire to smoke I did. There was no first time grace period for me because smoking out of a dented soda can I got extremely high the very first time. I remember everything moving in slow motion and having a feeling of being out of control. In fact the opposite was true but that was not the reality for me at the time.

Two events that I remember clearly about that night were as follows. Soon after we came in from a fairly impressive session I had my first taste of cotton mouth. So, logically I got up to get myself a soda. For some reason when I got to the soda I was somehow entranced by the beauty of the can and went back to where I was sitting without even getting the drink. Also, the munchies are a large part of the beginning smoker's habits. So that night I got myself a rice krispie treat took one bite decided it was too hard to chew and fell asleep with it lying next to my head.

I had created a reality of pure laziness where the simple act of chewing was too much of a hardship for me. If I had changed my frame of mind to that of having the best time of my life then that reality would have liberated me and I would have done just that. I have had many other experiences with THC enhanced plants since then and have gotten to the point of being able to have an awesome time every time. This is in no way an endorsement for smoking, but I do believe that you should trust what you know is "true" and make the decision from that state of mind.

Freshmen year continued on smoothly and I had a good time pretty much all the way through it. The only thing that kept me from being happy all the time was the fact that I was still feeling the need to impress people with either exaggerated or completely false tales. It was a constant strain on me to have to distort the truth in order to feel like I was fitting in. On the outside it did seem like I was fitting in and the summer after freshmen year was the best I had experienced so far.

Sophomore year started out much as the year before with excitement and almost immediate acceptance from a larger group of people. I was happy but still not true to myself. Not only did I make up stories and lie directly to people, I also at the same time was lying to the person inside that knew what I was doing was wrong.

Along with responsibility age tends to come with more freedom. I always wanted to be out and with all the people that I had come to be acquainted with. Although I did like being out I still was pretty reserved and did not think to talk unless I was sure I would get a desired reaction. I know now that if your intention is good you will always get the desired reaction. I continued this way all year just floating not having any real purpose or motivation other than to be accepted by a small group of people. I had no idea at that point that the goal itself was not wrong, but attaining it through false pretenses will not bring true satisfaction.

My year continued and people became more important to me than school which caused my grades to no longer reflect my intelligence. I never worried about this and continued to try and build meaningful relationships with a larger group of people. I was enjoying going to school only out of the satisfaction of making other people happy while in fact I should have wanted to be happy first. If I was true to myself, I would have had all that I wanted plus an inner peace which is worth more than anything else on this Earth.

The summer after that year, which in reality was only eight months ago, had a huge impact on my life up to this point. I reverted back to a substance that although had made me feel somewhat out of control at the same time I liked. This of course was good old sweet jeeba. I found that I could hang out with anyone I wanted if I provided the herbal refreshments. This was fine for me since I had a job and I liked getting ripped. That summer was probably the best time in my life up until about two weeks ago.

I got high everyday most of the time more than once a day and I loved every second of it. The truth was though that I was not at all content when I was not out with these people that I liked to be around so much. While I was at work or on vacation or anywhere else I was constantly restless and unsatisfied. The drug had control of me since I was not in the mental state to be in control of it. I felt I had to justify my actions, when in fact through justification I was admitting that I was not in control. If I had been true to myself and thought completely that it was the right thing for me to do then there would be no need to justify to anyone.

Through this whole time my parents were suspecting exactly what was happening because at the time they had a much stronger grasp on intuition than I did. My whole summer consisted of getting ripped and then trying to make it seem to my parents that I was not. This intent for deception was a huge burden on me at all times and I lost my appreciation for most things that I loved doing purely because I was wasting my energy trying to deceive my parents. Athletics and fitness have always been a huge part of the true me, and I was denying myself that so as to be able to smoke more.

I was in no means being true to myself, so I was in fact losing myself in a drug. Nothing seemed right if I was not high. This I know is a huge obstacle for many people who self-medicate on any number of substances, and I hope that through reading this book they will realize that they do not need any of it.

Junior year started out like a dream. The first weekend was three days long and there was a party every night. On top of that I had in my possession the headiest nuggets I had ever seen and was more than ready to go through all of them. I got more stoned that weekend than I ever had before and for a while it was the standard by which I measured all other weekends.

Shortly thereafter I was caught red eyed by my parents for the first time. I witnessed in a THC induced haze three eighths and 135 dollars get flushed down the toilet. I have to hold back the tears even while reminiscing right now. It was the first of many battles with my parents that would in the end lead up to the writing of this book.

My life was a constant battle to make people believe that I did not have a problem. But in fact, now that I realize that I did, it is no longer a problem at all. The constant justification of my actions was occupying nearly all of my mental energy and in turn my school work was drastically below where it had always been. I knew I needed some way to get inner peace I just didn't know how.

I got caught constantly and was grounded, drug tested, sent to therapy, and forced to do parental induced community service. All of which were the right things to do for me at the time. I found myself trying to be more honest and if I did lie then I would almost immediately admit that it was a joke. This felt better but was not complete. I still felt that I needed to lie so as to get high, and because of that every other task was made that much harder. I couldn't do school work, I had no desire to do anything around the house, and I only occasionally did any real physical activity. I was at the point where I had nothing to lose.

So one day I got caught and answered every question my parents had with as much honesty as I could. After having this monumental conversation they came to the conclusion that they could not stop me from doing what I wanted to do, so they gave me free reign at last. The only stipulations were that I had to do more around the house and always answer questions truthfully when asked. This was incredible for me and I knew with every intuition that this was the best course of action for my parents to take. Immediately my spirits rose and I started to be more outspoken, like I had been in my early years. The innocence was coming back. I did struggle for a short period of time, all of which has happened in just the past few weeks. Although I struggled, I remained true to myself. I knew with everything that things would work out exactly how I wanted them to.

I began and do tell the truth without hesitation, every time I did I liked it even more. This translated into contentment at all times where work in the house seemed effortless because it was a means of being able to go out and do what I truly wanted to do on the weekends. Since this plan has been in place I have talked to people more openly than ever before and have been able to articulate perfectly all that I know is good. I do not judge anyone for being different, I merely try and take something good from every person I meet. If you believe that people will not lie to you there is a better chance that they won't.

All that I have mentioned has lead up to the person today who lives every second with utter joy. I thrive off of seeing people start to question whether the assumed "traditional" methodologies are necessarily the correct ones. I have no doubt in my mind that I could not have reached this point without every event that has happened to me in my life. Undoubtedly the ability to tell the truth has always liberated me more than I could ever describe with words.

Made in the USA
Middletown, DE
07 March 2021

34221140R10104